CW01497372

MULTI-AXIS
SPINDLE TURNING

A Systematic Exploration

Barbara Dill

Schiffer Publishing Ltd

4880 Lower Valley Road • Atglen, PA 19310

Other Schiffer Books on Related Subjects:

New Woodturning Techniques and Projects: Advanced Level,
Helga Becker, Photography by Richard Becker, ISBN 978-0-7643-5018-4

Turning to Art in Wood: A Creative Journey,
The Center for Art in Wood, ISBN 978-0-7643-4204-2

Spalted Wood: The History, Science, and Art of a Unique Material,
Sara C. Robinson, Hans Michaelsen & Julia C. Robinson, ISBN 978-0-7643-5038-2

Copyright © 2018 by Barbara Dill

Library of Congress Control Number: 2017955737

All rights reserved. No part of this work may be reproduced or used in any form or
by any means—graphic, electronic, or mechanical, including photocopying or
information storage and retrieval systems—without written permission
from the publisher.

The scanning, uploading, and distribution of this book or any part thereof via the
Internet or any other means without the permission of the publisher is illegal and
punishable by law. Please purchase only authorized editions and do not
participate in or encourage the electronic piracy of copyrighted materials.

"Schiffer," "Schiffer Publishing, Ltd.," and the pen and inkwell logo are registered
trademarks of Schiffer Publishing, Ltd.

Cover design by Justin Watkinson
Type set in ConduitITC & Minion

ISBN: 978-0-7643-5534-9
Printed in China

Published by Schiffer Publishing, Ltd.
4880 Lower Valley Road
Atglen, PA 19310
Phone: (610) 593-1777; Fax: (610) 593-2002
E-mail: Info@schifferbooks.com
Web: www.schifferbooks.com

For our complete selection of fine books on this and related subjects, please visit
our website at www.schifferbooks.com. You may also write for a free catalog.

Schiffer Publishing's titles are available at special discounts for bulk purchases for
sales promotions or premiums. Special editions, including personalized covers,
corporate imprints, and excerpts, can be created in large quantities for special
needs. For more information, contact the publisher.

We are always looking for people to write books on new and related subjects. If
you have an idea for a book, please contact us at proposals@schifferbooks.com.

To my wife and best friend, Shelly Klinger, who has encouraged me
and supported me on this amazing exploration; and to Sid Morton,
who was my carving teacher in the late '80s and who
encouraged me all along the way. I am grateful.

CONTENTS

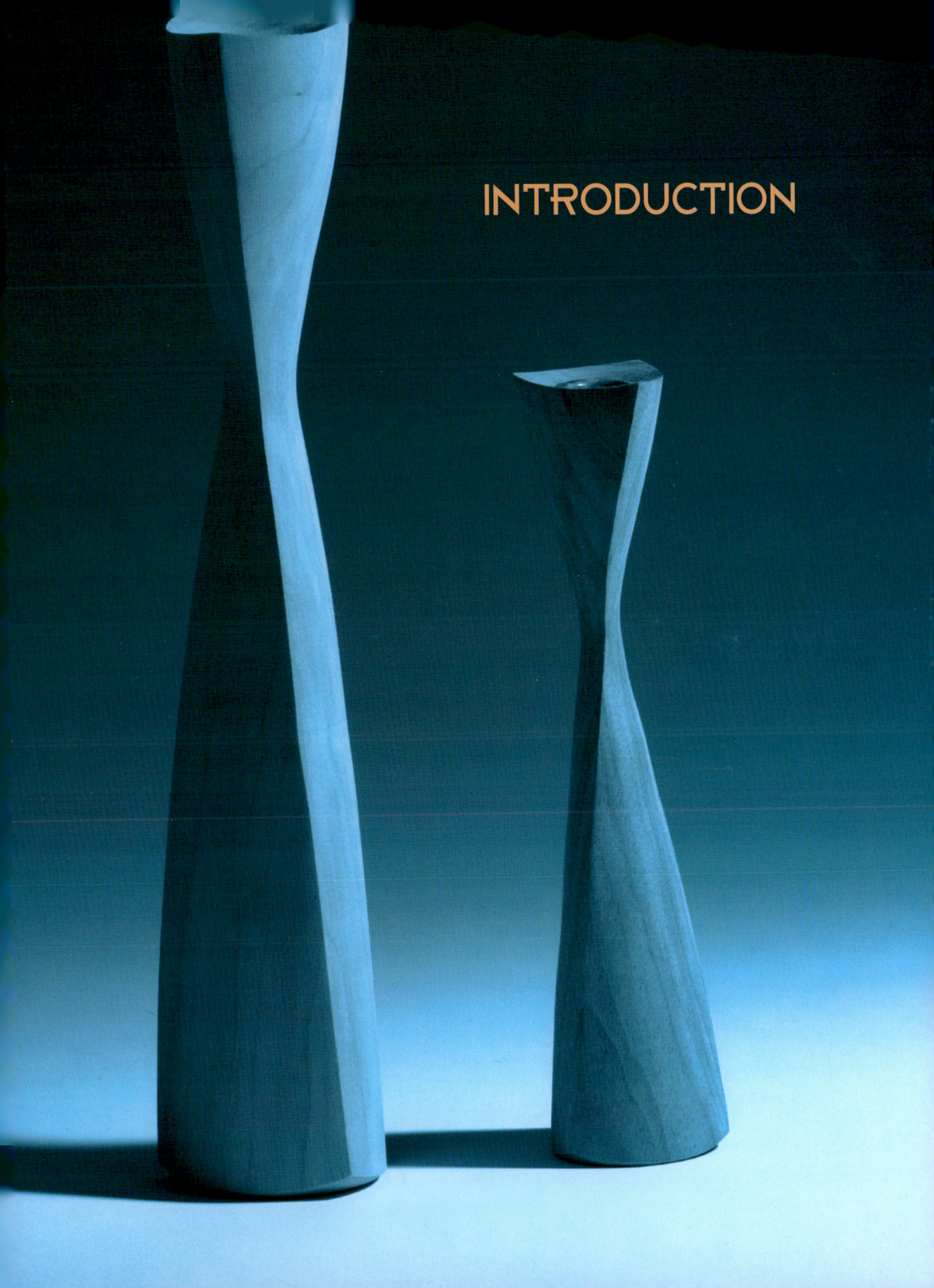

INTRODUCTION

The process of turning a spindle on more than one axis can be quite confusing. I first really noticed multi-axis turnings in 1993, at a world turning conference. I was intrigued and couldn't wait to try this myself. The image above shows some of my first attempts at multi-axis turnings.

The middle one is my first experiment. I thought that the angles between axes surely must be very large to create such amazing forms. I'm lucky that I still have all of my fingers. Most of the forms I could find were made by moving the axis to a random second and/or third axis and then creating a bead or cove or a v-cut. Notice that even though I had turned many forms, I had no idea how to think about them or to think about what to do next. I was confused and discouraged.

For a time, I stopped playing with multi-axis spindles. The few turners who taught this way of turning would explain the mechanics or steps that were involved in creating one of their designs. If my notes were good enough and if I could get into my shop right away, I could turn the things that were shown to me. This did not help me learn what to do next! The few articles and books that had been written were helpful, but didn't explain these ideas in a way that really helped me break through to another level of understanding.

In 2006, I challenged myself to figure out how to think about multi-axis turning. I sensed that there must be a way to group spindles that were similar and then figure out what they had in common. I was tired of the random "hit or miss" method. I started understanding how these spindles were related. It took me a long time to understand

and remember these ideas and years to organize the ideas in a logical sequence. My first attempts at teaching this to others were clumsy at best. But I was amazed at the feedback I received at the end of these early demonstrations. Often I was told that this demo was the best explanation they had ever heard about off-center turning. These comments encouraged me to continue this exploration.

There are many ways to create asymmetrical forms using the lathe. My focus has been on spindle turning, rather than face plate turning. My exploration has included simply finding what can happen between centers, meaning between the headstock and the tailstock, when changing the axis. This area of turning is certainly complex and confusing. A systematic approach is essential. I refer to myself as an experimental turner. Finding a form spurs me on to experimenting further. I continue to think of ideas that I have not yet tried.

The lathe is a carving tool. For most of us, using more than one axis is a fun and exciting way to carve wood on the lathe. Multi-axis, eccentric, multi-centered, angular turning, thermed turning, and split turning are some, but not all, of these words used to describe this work.

Pleasing asymmetrical forms are often found by experimentation and by luck.

This book will help you to understand the area of multi-axis spindle turning; to gain a simple vocabulary that works to explain these concepts; to organize these ideas so that you can understand the wealth of options available.

The last chapter is a focus on those other woodturners, both past and present, who have made such an impact on the world of wood turning, sculpture, and art.

How to Use This Information

The framework presented here has helped me and many others who want to create asymmetrical objects using the lathe as a carving tool. Knowing how these spindles are related has pointed to many ideas that I had never thought of before. This framework provides a vocabulary necessary for us all to communicate about multi-axis turning. It offers an alternative to copying the work of others. It offers paths that have yet to be discovered. It is a systematic way of thinking that is a teaching tool.

It is my hope that this information provides a basis for thinking and exploration and that more clarity will grow from these ideas.

Many turners have creatively found beautiful and/or interesting forms using multiple axes. This theoretical framework allows any woodturner to systematically explore multi-axis turning. *Each spindle made is a building block for future ideas. This exploration is one way to then create a body of work.*

I think it is very important for a person to start by making spindles from each quadrant . . . that is, to start at the beginning. Spending time understanding more simple forms will help when the urge to create a masterpiece can't be resisted. Once spindles are created, they can be saved for future reference. Understanding and seeing happens over time and is a path to finding your own creative voice. And, yes, it takes hours of playful experimentation to develop not only the needed skills, but a true understanding of this area of turning.

As Derek Weidman said when asked how he visualizes the intricate sculptures that he creates, "it is the intuition attained from persistent experimentation" (p. 50, *American Woodturner*, December 2015).

A Brief History

My journey as a woodturner began in 1990. Michael Hosaluk was my teacher at Arrowmont that summer. Since I had no idea what a headstock or tailstock was, my focus was on turning a symmetrical piece of wood safely. Using more than one axis was not even a part of my awareness then.

I attended a World Turning Symposium in 1993, and saw multi-axis turnings from Europe as well as the States. It was then that I really started noticing Michael Hosaluk and Mark Sfirri's work. I was always fascinated and curious about how they did what they did using multiple axes. The few articles that I could find written about multi-axis turning in the 1990s were written by Mark Sfirri, followed by a book by Ray Hopper, *Multi-Centre Woodturning*, in 1992, and an article by Sigi Angerer in 1998, "Angular Turning on the Lathe."

As I started going to high end craft shows, like the American Craft Council shows, I noticed Stoney Lamar and his work. He did amazing large pieces using more than one axis on the lathe.

From Ray Hopper's book, I learned that the axes can be placed anywhere on a rectangular piece of wood, even the sides. He clearly demonstrated how to make oval tool handles and then fruits and even a performing seal.

Sigi Angerer's article is about angular turning. His angular turnings referred to the turnings that I now refer to as split turnings and thermed turnings. He references a book published in 1756 called *The Turning Art* written by Martin Teuber. He also cites a book written by Hugo Knoppe called *The Turner's Handbook*, which was written in the 1800s.

Mike Darlow published his first comprehensive book on wood turning in 1985. His second book, published in 1999, *Woodturning Methods*, has a chapter about eccentric turning and one on multi-axis turning. His research finds that the earliest reference regarding therming is in a book written by Bergeron called the *Manuel du Tourneur*. He noted that therming has been referenced in some German texts but it has barely been mentioned in English turning books. He also included a discussion of angular, skewed, and inside out turning.

Although using more than one axis has been used for many years, it is the work of Ray Hopper, Mark Sfirri, Stoney Lamar, Jean-François Escoulen, and others that have made popular the sculptural possibilities of using more than one axis while turning.

Peter Exton took therming to a new level in the early 2000s. He began turning in 1990 and was fascinated with split turnings also known as reverse turning or inside out turning. He discovered using diamonds for turning. His work is fascinating and groundbreaking.

Tom Crabb did amazing pieces using the lathe as a basis for his work. His work was mostly side grain and bias work rather than spindle work. He had a very positive and encouraging influence on me as I sought to discover ways to understand multi-axle spindle turning.

There are many other turners whose work was not noticed by me then, but is now in my world view. And since the early 2000s, an online search will reveal that there are many more references about these techniques and the many turners who are exploring them.

Skills

Having the skill to turn beads and coves and v-cuts on one axis really helps when turning on multiple axes! These skills are developed by hours of playful and systematic experimentation on the lathe.

The skills required to make multi-axis turnings are the same skills needed to turn a spindle on one axis. The mechanics of using a spindle gouge are similar to the use of other tools used to make beads and v-cuts. The bevel of the spindle gouge rides on the wood, keeping the tip high on the wood and the tool pointed slightly in the direction of the turn. When making a bead, roll the tool to the right, point the tool to the right, and use the right tip to cut the wood. The tool is pointed to the left and the left tip is used when cutting to the left, as seen on the next page. The bevel must ride on the wood to create the utmost control and success of the cut. Keeping the bevel on the wood also keeps the tip high on the wood. The arrows in the picture point out the area of the spindle gouge to use.

Tools

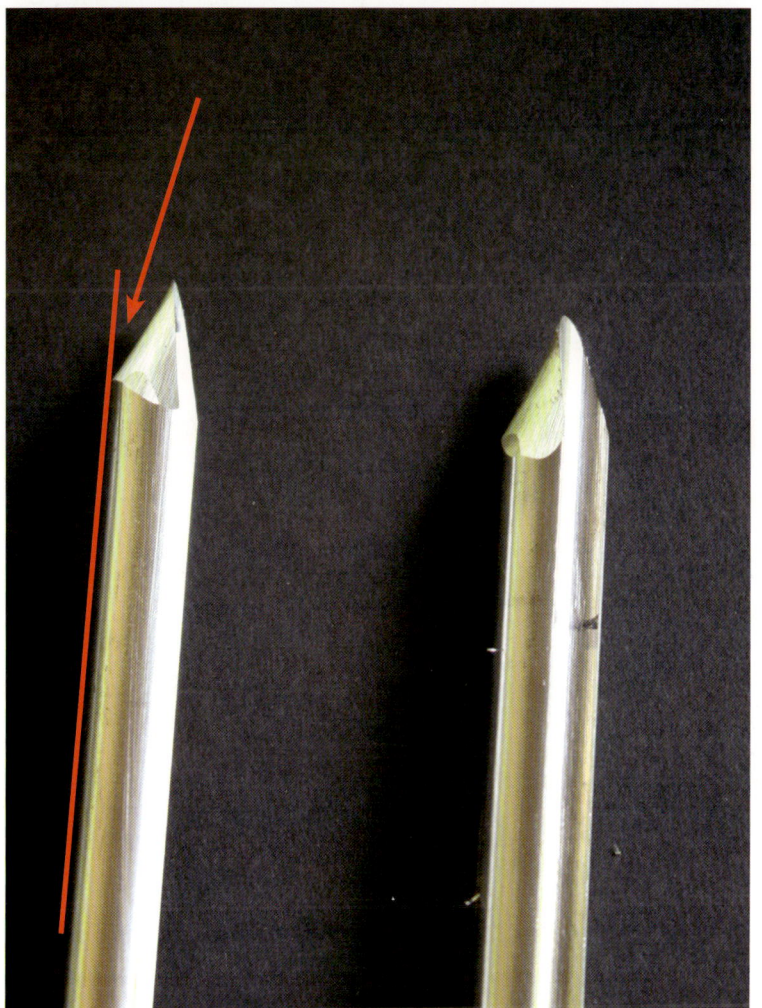

This is a half-inch spindle gouge. The red arrow points to the thirty degree angle.

Every turner has preferences and reasons for their preferences regarding tools. Whatever tool you use to cut a profile reliably is the correct tool for you to use for multi-axis work. And whatever drive center or tool rest or live tail center that you use successfully is also correct.

The tools that I use ninety-nine percent of the time are the half-inch spindle gouge and the half-inch deep fluted bowl gouge sharpened like a spindle roughing gouge. I use the tool that makes the smoothest cut. I also experiment with different ways to sharpen a tool if I'm having trouble with a specific cut.

I use a half-inch spindle gouge. The spindle gouge has a fingernail grind. This grind is perfect for making v-cuts and beads. Others may use a skew or another tool. The spindle gouge is sharpened to about thirty degrees off of the tool bar. The angle on this grind can vary depending on the required cut. For instance, if the v-cut is deep and steep, the tool can be sharpened accordingly. The control of the cut is improved when the tool rest and the tool are kept as close to the work as possible. Detail gouges are spindle gouges that have more metal in the shaft. I have used both and now prefer the spindle gouge.

Most woodturners now use a sharpening jig of some sort to keep the tools sharp and the angles true. These images show the different angles the Wolverine jig is set to for the spindle gouge and the bowl gouge. The left-hand image shows the angle used to sharpen the half-inch spindle gouge. Notice the angle that the Wolverine jig is set to for making

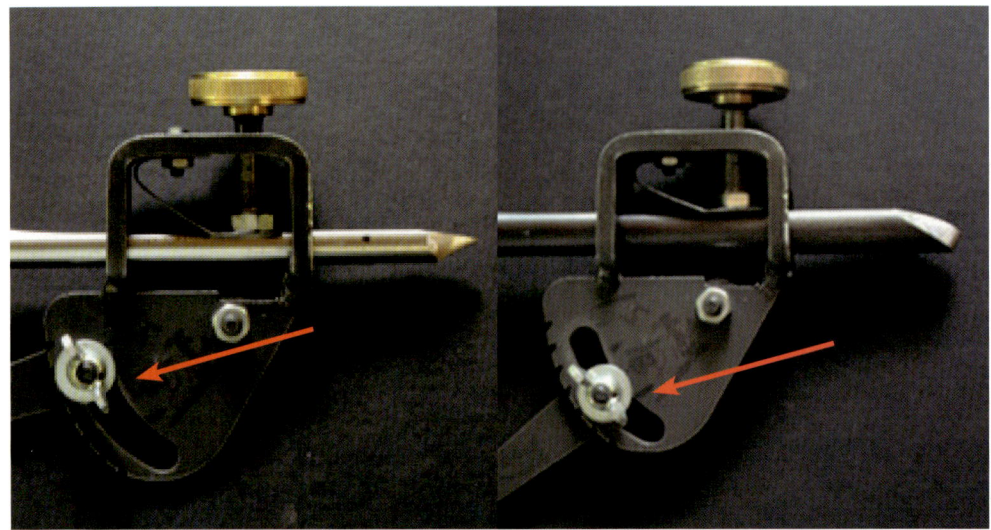

Position of jig when sharpening a spindle gouge   Position of jig when sharpening a bowl gouge

the fingernail grind on the spindle gouge. This angle is different from the one used to make the classic bowl grind (above right). *These angles and methods of sharpening each tool can be changed to solve a problem while turning.*

I use a half-inch deep fluted bowl gouge for roughing as well as turning long beads and coves. The bowl gouge is sharpened like a spindle-roughing gouge. It is flat on the cutting edge and sharpened at about a forty-five degree angle.

There are a few ways to sharpen this roughing gouge. I usually place the end of the handle in the v arm support of the Wolverine jig and adjust the angle on the sharpening wheel.

Half-inch deep fluted bowl gouge sharpened like a roughing gouge. It is flat on the cutting edge and sharpened at a forty-five degree angle.

Another way is to set the platform to a forty-five degree angle and keep the handle perpendicular to the grinding wheel.

This is a half-inch bowl gouge sharpened by using the same angle on the sharpening jig that I use for a spindle gouge. I use this tool for many cuts that require a heavier tool than the spindle gouge. The weight of the tool provides a bit more stability than a spindle gouge provides while making some cuts. This is

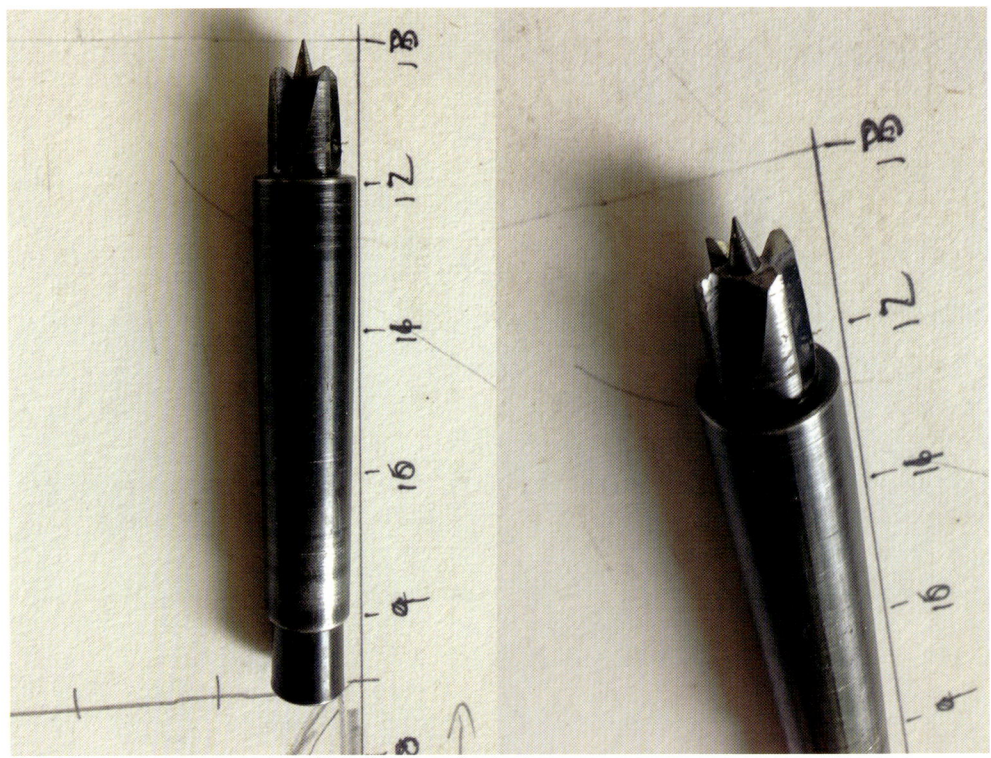

an example of thinking outside of the box and sharpening a tool in an unconventional way to help with a specific need.

I use a four-prong drive center that has a half-inch diameter for most of the smaller spindles that I turn. I prefer using a larger four-prong drive center when and if the smaller center drills into the wood. This can happen when the wood is soft and when using green wood. I like the way that the prongs bite into the wood, even if the angle is such that only two prongs are pushed into the wood. Other options are safety drives or Steb centers with a spring-loaded point. I have found that I can use less pressure with less spin out when using the four-prong centers. Note that there is no right or wrong tool to use. We all have become accustomed to various tools through the years. It is critical to have consistently good results with whatever tool you use.

Heavier lathes help decrease the vibration that happens when turning an off balanced piece of wood. Lathe speed is important when making cuts that involve air wood, meaning that the tool contacts the wood only part of the time, resulting in a tendency to bounce. The faster the speed, the less bounce there is when making interrupted cuts. The weight of the wood limits the speed of the turning due to excess vibration when the speed is increased. Speed is a safety issue as well. Never use a speed that feels unsafe to you.

Lighting is important. A light that is directly over the work highlights the air wood effectively. To see more clearly, use a background that is either white or black, depending on the color of the wood being turned.

Safety is very important. Wearing a face shield and letting nothing dangle from your clothing or body, like long hair or loose fabric that could get entwined in a spinning object, are some factors to consider. My rule of thumb is to always be well rested, focused on my work, and free from medications that might interfere with my judgment/safety.

Wood

The woods used for wood turning are generally hardwoods. The choice that must be made is whether to use green wood or dried wood. I live in an area of the country where beautiful hardwoods are plentiful. I enjoy turning green wood unless I am creating a form that will check due to its thickness. I was lucky to have had a huge red oak tree fall on my land just when I began to explore multi-axis turning. I had free wood to experiment with. Turning green wood us usually less dusty and is more forgiving when mastering the tools.

There are many colors of wood available in the forest. I have found that the lighter woods show the delicate intersection of each axis and the shadows that are created. Holly, maple, and ash are perfect woods for this type of turning. That being said, I love the richness of the darker woods. I have turned many forms from walnut and mulberry with great results. All in all, the choice of wood to be used becomes a personal preference.

Definition of Terms

I will stay away from mathematical equations when explaining things, so that your eyes don't glaze over like mine usually do. I prefer using logic when explaining how to think about these ideas. I also will use many photos and drawings to illustrate the ideas. The following terms are used frequently, so I'll define them now.

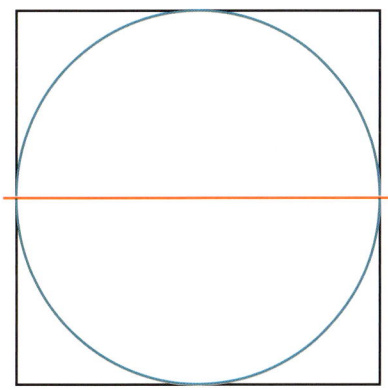

The diameter of a square or a circle is a straight line through the center to each side.

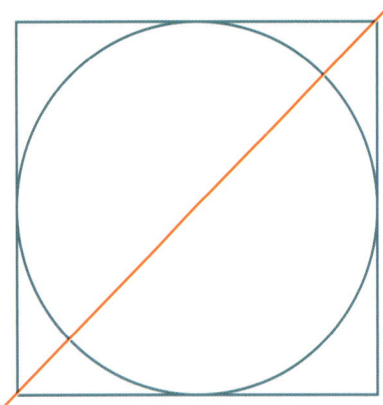

The diagonal of a square is the distance from one corner to the opposite corner.

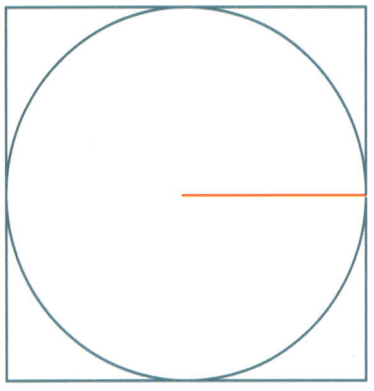

The radius is the distance from the center of a circle to the outside circumference of that circle. The radius of a square is half of its diameter.

Parallel lines are the same distance apart. No matter how far they extend they will never meet. Non-parallel lines converge or cross each other at some point. In this application, each type of axis is defined by its *relationship to the center axis*. Non-parallel axes are referred to as *twisted axes* because of the resulting visual twist that occurs in the spindle.

Any time an axis is moved from the center axis, as it spins, some of the wood between the headstock and tailstock looks like solid wood and some of the wood looks like it has air in it. I have called these the "solid wood" and the "air wood." Other names for the "air wood" are "ghost wood" and "blurry wood."

Solid wood   Air wood

1
BASIC CONCEPTS

The key to unraveling this confusing method of turning wood is quite simple. There are two basic observations that are critical in formulating a way to organize the many variables and outcomes into a systematic way to understand multi-axis spindle turning. These ideas can apply to each segment of a new axis or the entire spindle.

#1 Axis Placement

There are only two ways that the new axis can be moved *relative to the center axis*: *parallel* or *nonparallel (twisted)*.

In other words, is the new axis parallel to the center (or not)? Each type of axis is defined by its relationship to the center axis.

A parallel axis is parallel to the center axis of the spindle or any line parallel to that center axis.

This means that when making a new axis, both ends are moved the same distance and in the same direction from the center axis. These drawings illustrate two of many options for the placement of parallel axes.

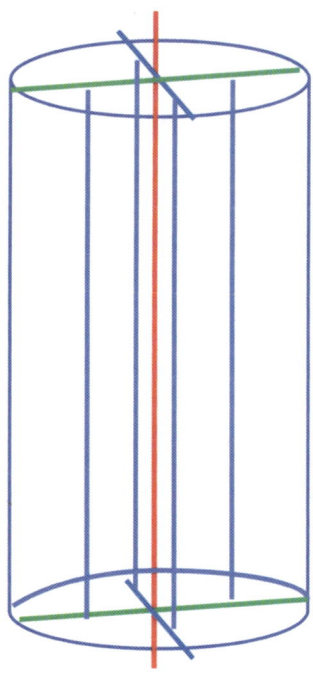

A twisted or nonparallel axis intersects the center axis of the spindle or any line parallel to the center axis at some point in time. It is called "twisted" due to the resulting visual twist. These drawings illustrate three of many options for the placement of twisted axes.

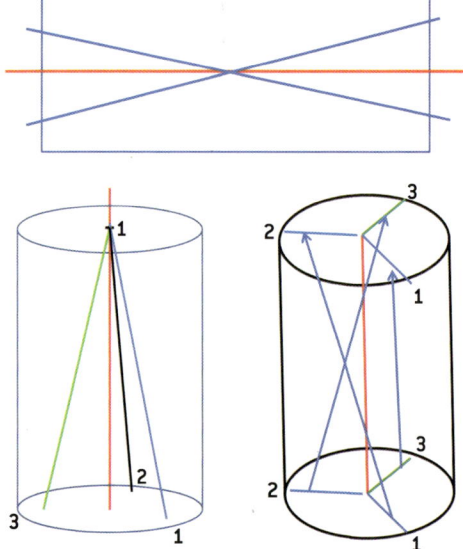

#2 Outcome

There are only two results that can happen when the axis is moved from the center axis to a new axis: *arc type* and *circular type.*

These two types of spindles refer to not only the visual differences, but also the cross sections of each type. When turning, the cuts are made through the air wood and into the solid wood, creating a *cylinder* (circular type), or the cuts are made into the air wood, creating an *arc* (arc type). It is easy to understand the cross section by thinking about slices of a cucumber.

Arc type

Circular type

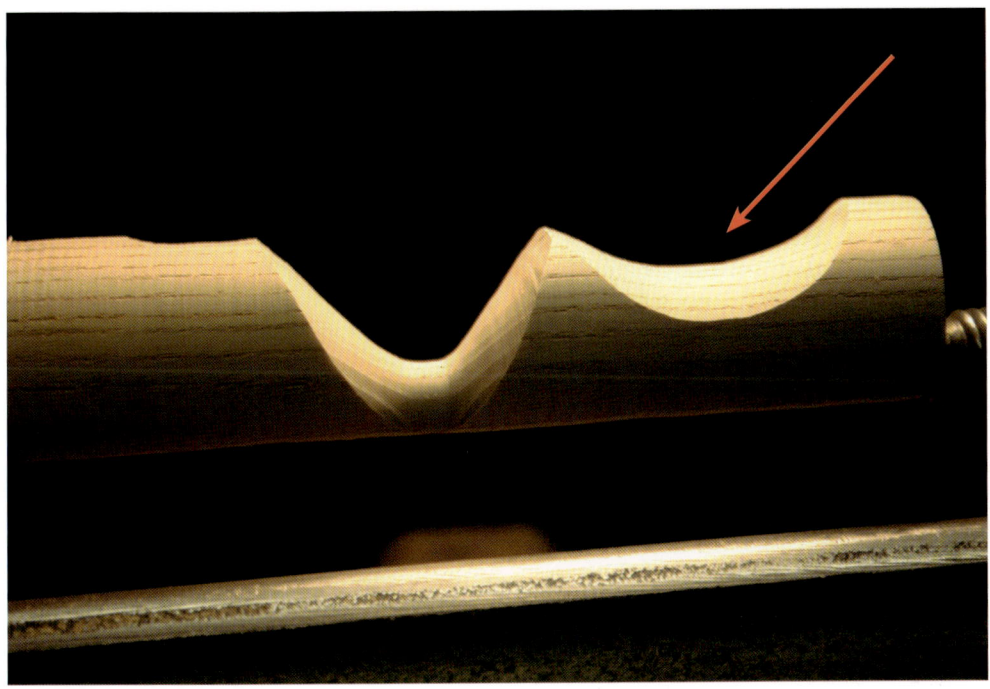

Arc types occur when the new profile is cut into the air wood or ghost wood, never reaching the solid wood of the new axis.

There are times when a cut, usually the first cut, enters the solid wood. However, after the other axes are cut, an arc type spindle will emerge. Ending the cut with the tip of the tool partially engaging with air produces an arc in the cross section of the spindle.

The profiles of each axis intersect, creating an arc type outcome. The intersection of these profiles forms lines lengthwise on the spindle. The intersection of these profiles is also seen by viewing a cross section or a slice. The horizontal cross section is arc shaped (below left). The radius from the new axis creates this arc (below right).

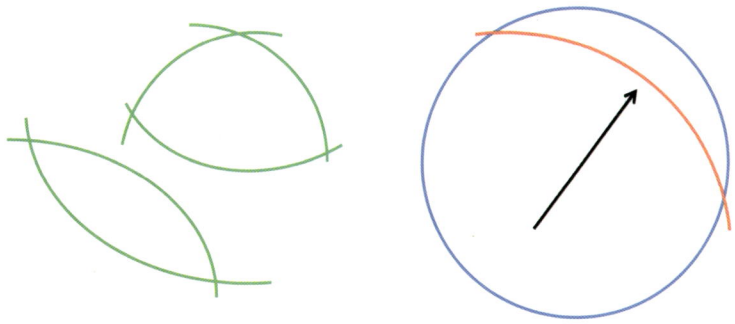

Here are examples of an arc type spindle. The image on the left has been made using parallel axes. The one on the right was made using twisted axes. The drawing shows how the axes were positioned.

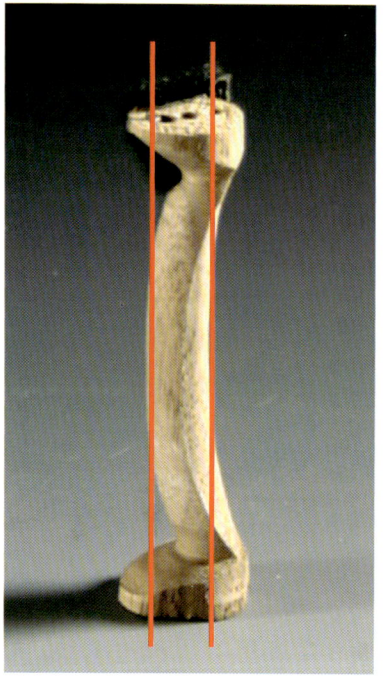
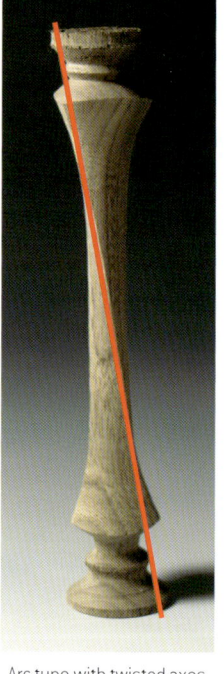
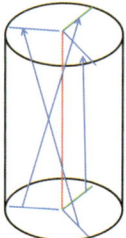

Arc type with parallel axes

Arc type with twisted axes

Circular types occur when a cut is made through the air wood to the new solid wood of the new axis.

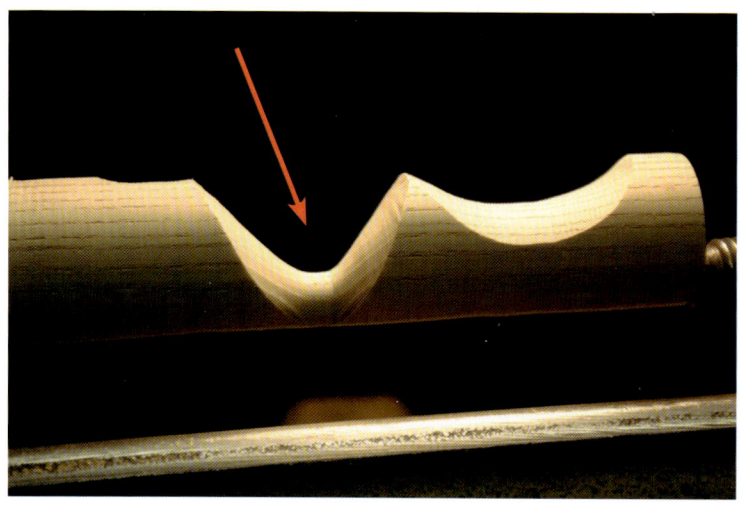

Ending the cut with the tip of the tool in the new solid wood produces a turned cylinder. The shape of the spindle is smooth and circular. When turning a parallel axis, the horizontal cross section is circular. This is because the new cut is deep enough to go to the new "solid wood" and create a new cylinder on which a profile can be turned. If horizontal slices were taken from the spindle, this would be seen clearly. When turning a twisted axis, the horizontal cross section is oval. The radius from the new axis creates this circular or oval shape.

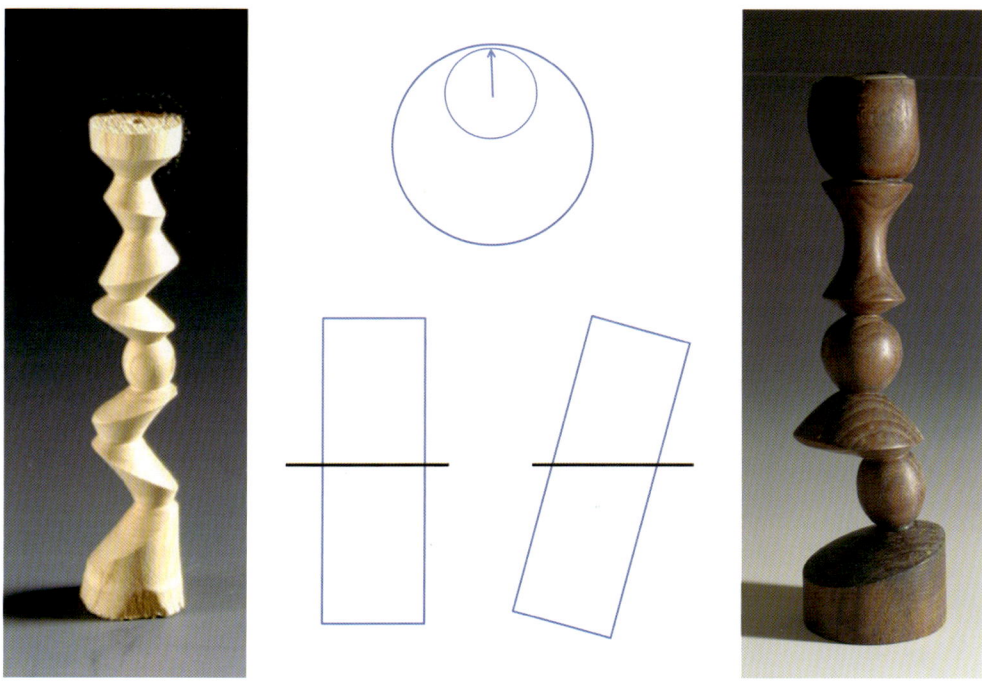

Circular type with parallel axes   Circular type with twisted axes

As these ideas unfold, you will see that *each type of axis placement is found in either type of outcome.* In other words, arc type and/or circular type can have parallel and/or twisted axes.

How the Arc and Circular Types Evolve

This is a visual description showing how each type of multi-axis spindle evolves. The details about the ideas and methods used are discussed at length in the following chapters. However, it is important to see this *now* to add to your understanding of these basic concepts.

This is an example of an arc type spindle with two parallel axes that are in the same plane of the center axis and are closer to the outside of the spindle.

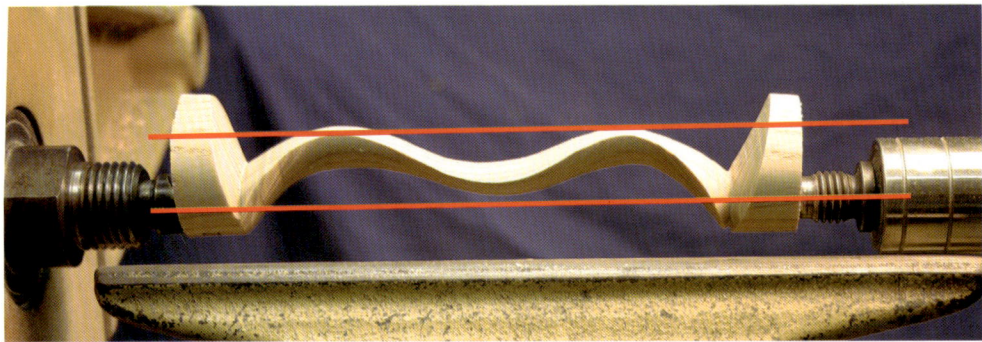

To prepare the spindle, turn the blank to a cylinder. Keep about one half inch of solid wood at each end. This provides space for clearly marking the axes and enough wood to prevent the wood from splitting while turning each axis. It also provides enough wood to save so that it is clear how that spindle was made and provides enough wood to make it into a project of your choice. Once you decide the placement of the new axes, vigorously press the new axes between the headstock and the tailstock while the spindle is not fragile. These holes let you use less pressure when the spindle is thin and more fragile. Now the spindle is ready to be turned. The red arrows point to the new axes.

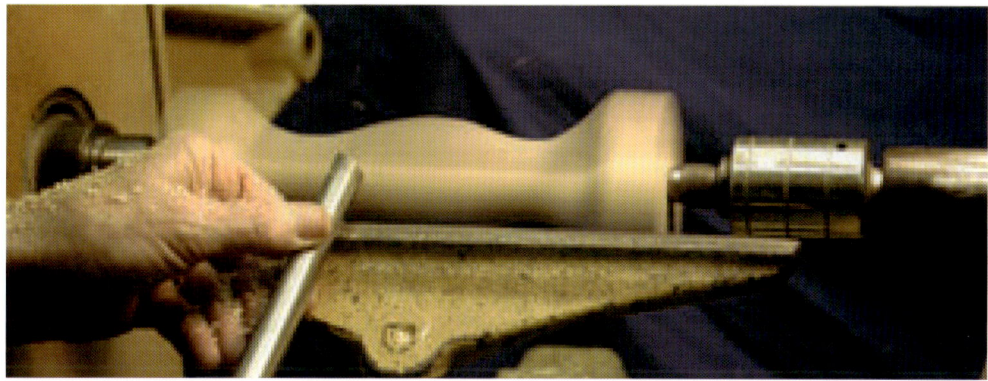

The first profile is turned into the air wood. A cove, a bead, and a cove are turned on this axis.

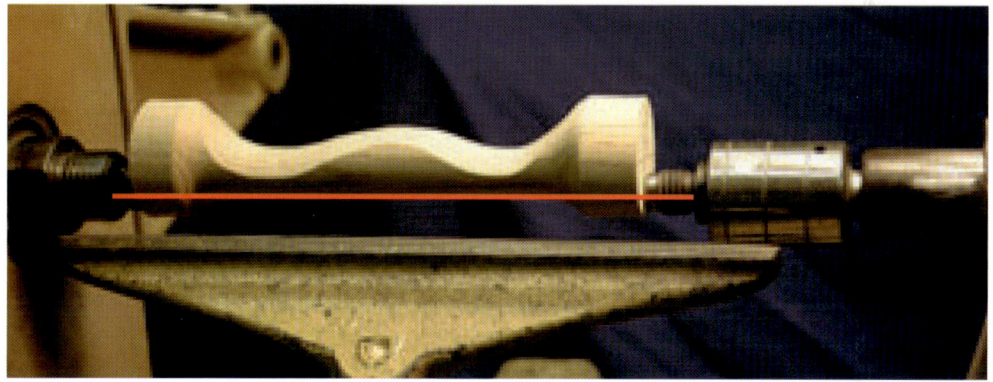

This image clearly shows the axis used between centers and the completed first profile.

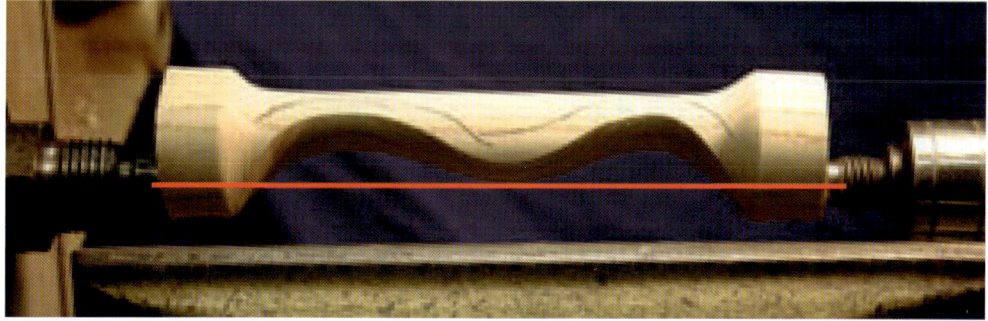

Now the spindle is moved to the second axis.

This image shows the lack of solid wood between the headstock and tailstock. This clearly demonstrates the importance of pressing the points of the head- and tailstock into the ends when the wood is solid.

A sketch of the intended profile can be drawn on the wood as a visual reminder. The only way to really see what is being turned is to stop the lathe often and look.

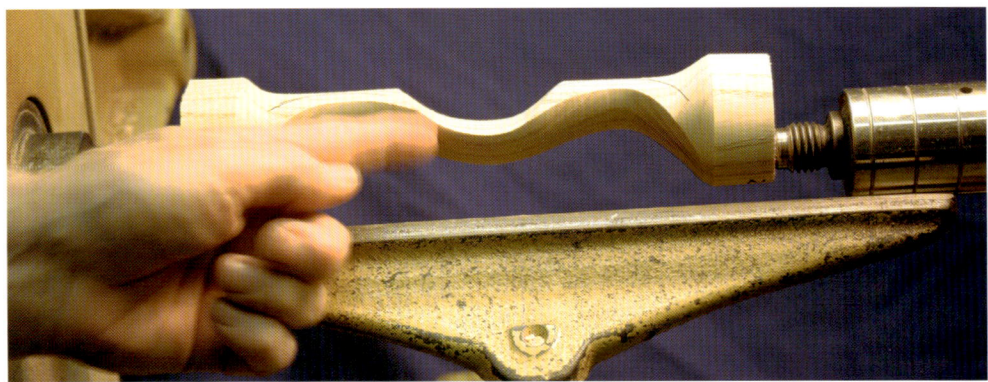

On this axis, a cove is turned first.

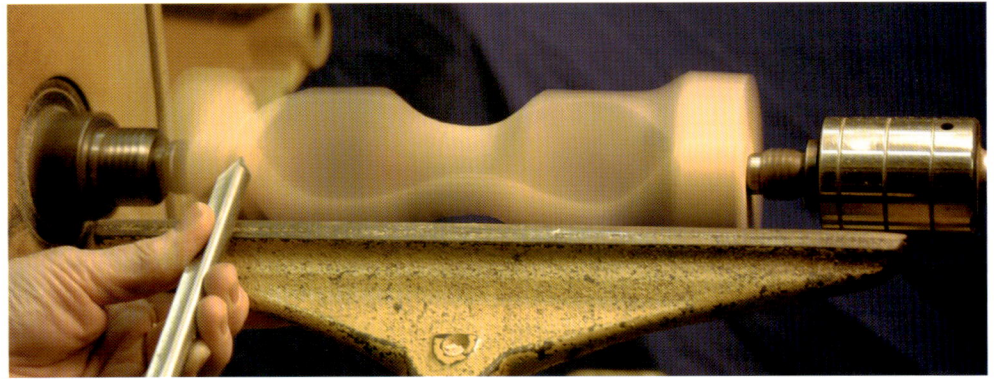

A bead is started on the left of the spindle by cutting a v-cut and then rounding the wood into the v-cut. The same cut is made on the right end.

How the Circular Type Evolves

This spindle has three twisted axes. On one end, the axes are separated by 120 degrees and are located closer to the center axis of the spindle and the same distance from the center axis (see bottom photo). The center axis is used on the other end.

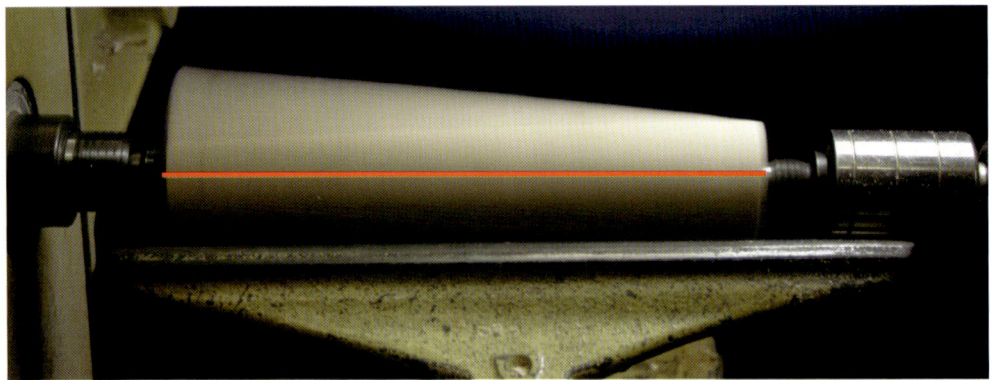

The air wood and the solid wood can be seen as the spindle is turning on the first axis. There is less air wood on the tailstock end since the point of the new axes is the center point on that end.

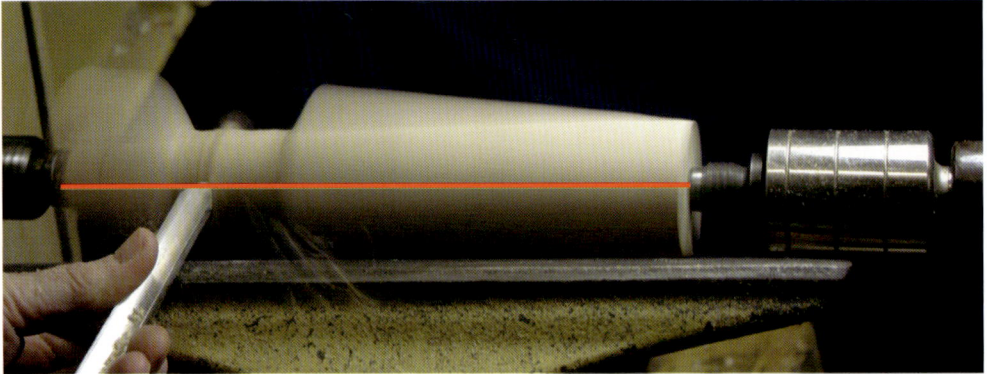

The cut has gone through the air wood and a cylinder has been made on the solid wood.

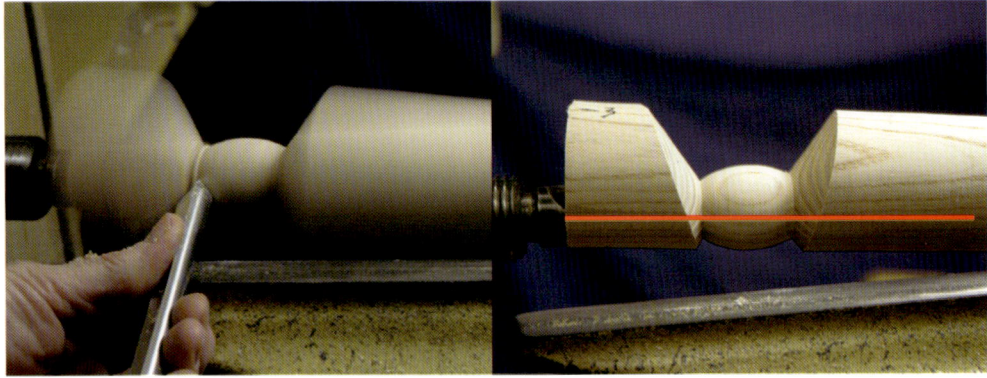

A bead is the profile turned on the cylinder.

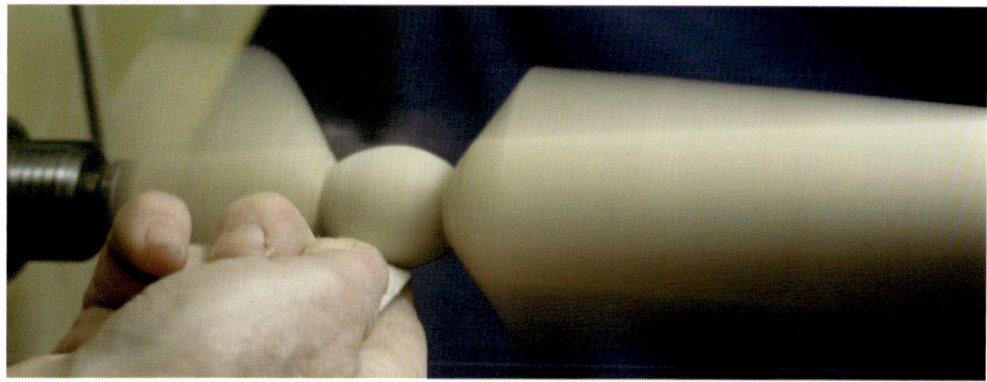

A safe way to sand a circular type spindle is to keep both hands on the front side of the lathe. Use care to avoid the air wood from hitting fingers and knuckles.

Now the spindle has been moved to the second axis. This image is another example of why it is important to press the holes into the wood before the spindle becomes fragile.

Again, a cylinder is defined by cutting through the air wood.

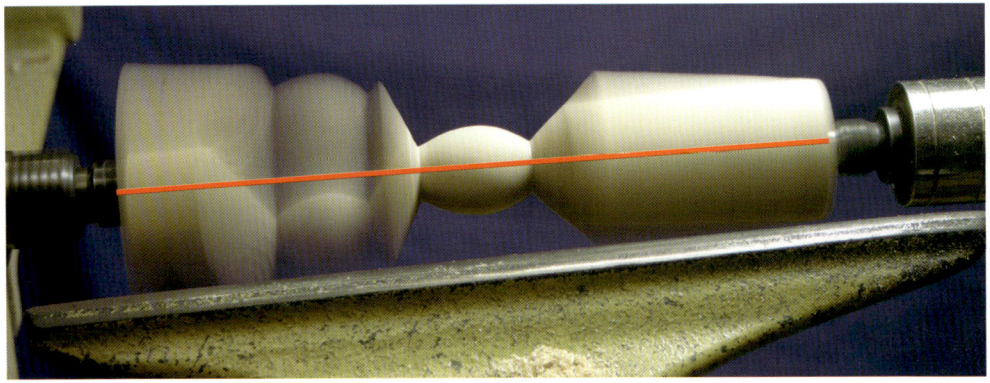

A bead is turned on that cylinder.

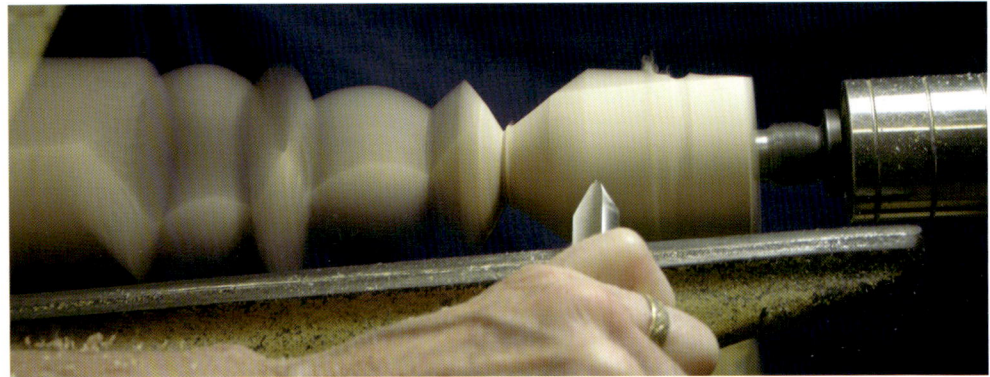

The profile of the third axis is a v-cut that captures the solid wood. Notice the shadows of the other two axes.

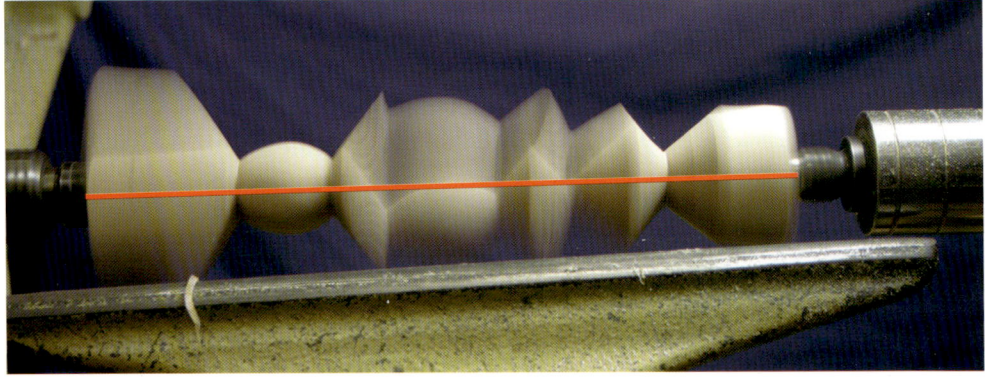

The spindle is now on the first axis used making the bead on the first axis visible. A v-cut is turned on this axis.

It's important to remember that a spindle can be created using both arc and circular outcomes. *The spindles shown here are totally arc or circular type for clarity.*

How to Organize This Information

In the world of science and mathematics, tables are often used to show how certain attributes are related. Once I isolated the two basic concepts (the two ways a new axis can be placed relative to the center axis and the two basic outcome types), I then visualized a table made of two lines that intersected at ninety degrees, thus creating four quadrants or separate areas.

The two outcome types are on the top line, with columns underneath. The two types of axis placement are placed on the side with columns going to the side. As these columns intersect, the four quadrants are seen. Each quadrant contains one type of axis placement and one type of outcome type.

In this table, all spindles that have parallel axes and are arc type are a family, meaning that they are similar. They are in quadrant 1.

Quadrant 2 contains spindles that have nonparallel or twisted axes and are arc type.

Quadrant 3 contains spindles that have parallel axes and are circular type.

Quadrant 4 contains spindles that have twisted axes and are circular type.

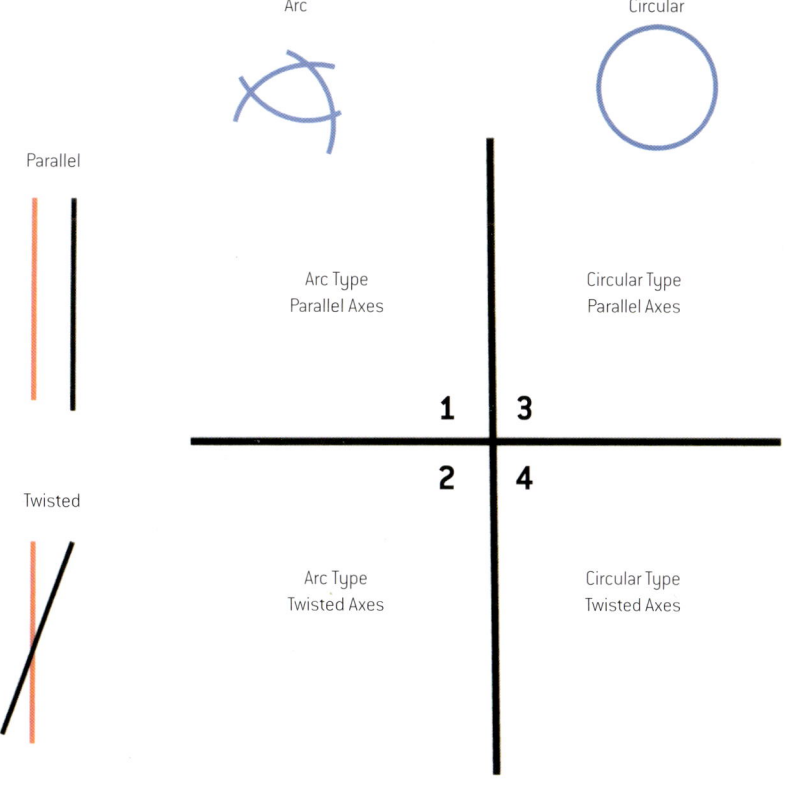

Arc

Circular

Parallel

Arc Type
Parallel Axes

Circular Type
Parallel Axes

1 | 3

2 | 4

Twisted

Arc Type
Twisted Axes

Circular Type
Twisted Axes

Now there is a way to think about how to arrange an axis and what type of spindle to turn.

In other words, the four basic families are the consequence of two considerations: are the axes parallel to the center axis (or not); and does the tip of the gouge stay in the wood (or not) at the end of its cut. Understanding these four families helps you envision an outcome. And those outcomes are hardly limited: each family comprises *countless* variations including type/size of wood used, the placement of the new axes, and the curvature of the cut.

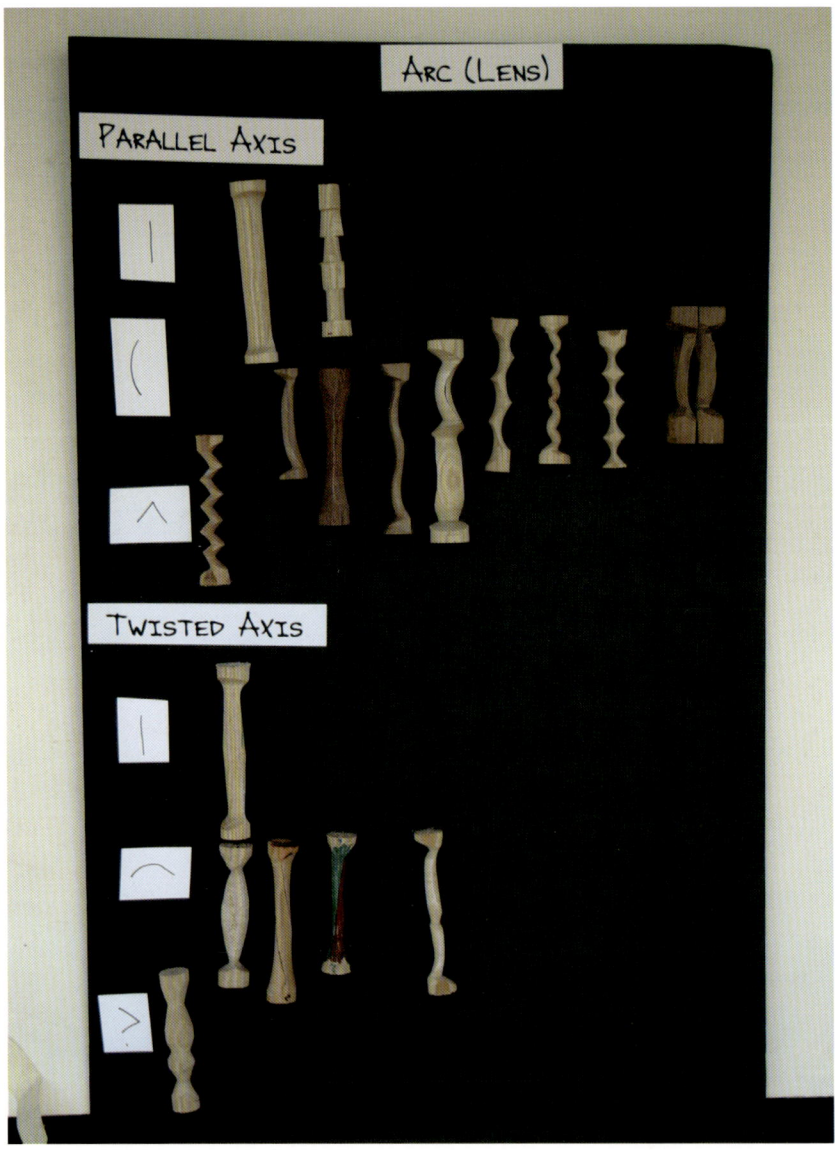

When I first created it, this table gave me ideas to try; so rather than running out of ideas as I had done in the past, I started filling in each quadrant and finding forms that I had never thought of before. These are the boards that I used to categorize the spindles. Most of the spindles that I had turned by randomly changing the axes were in the 4th quadrant . . . circular type and twisted or nonparallel axes.

I started waking up many mornings with a "what if I . . ." kind of idea that I had never thought of before. So understanding these ideas allowed me to decide the type of axes and the type of outcome I would make, meaning I had a starting point from which I could experiment with the many other variables inherent to spindle turning. With this theoretical framework and vocabulary, you can too.

OUTCOME/RESULTS

ARC TYPE   CIRCULAR TYPE

VARIABLES
PARALLEL AXIS
(Does not cross the
center axis.)

1   3

TWISTED AXIS
(Crosses the center axis or any line
parallel to the center axis.)

2   4

MANY OTHER VARIABLES EXIST IN
ALL QUADRANTS:

PROFILE: (straight, curved or v-cut)
symmetry, depth of cut.

AXES: Number of axes used; the
many options of axis placement;
distance of new axis from center;
various ways to connect the axes.

WOOD: Size and shape of wood;
orientation of wood to lathe

Why is this table significant? Before this information became clear, I relied on intuition, luck, and random experimentation to find intriguing forms. We now have a systematic way to think about multi-axis spindle turning. Now you can start with an idea about axis placement and the size of the wood and then intentionally experiment with the evolving form.

We now have a vocabulary to use when sharing ideas about multi-axis turnings. For example, rather than saying "the axis closest to you," now I can say "the axis is parallel and closer to the outside of the spindle." Using our shared understanding of this framework, together with our shared vocabulary, we can now turn to learning how to think about multi-axis turning more effectively. You can begin to create your own designs based on your own exploration of the limitless variables.

This is the basic framework. Yes, it does become more complex. There are many variables that apply to all aspects of spindle turning, variables that yield a symphony of possible outcomes that are yet to be found. These variables are discussed in depth in chapter three.

2
THE 4 QUADRANTS OF FAMILIES
OF MULTI-AXIS SPINDLES

(The Spindles within Each Quadrant)

Now that the details about the outcomes and the axes have been laid out, we return to the table and examine each quadrant. The spindles that are shown are internally congruent with each quadrant. This means that each entire spindle is made from the type of axis and outcome found in that quadrant. The spindles shown will illustrate only a few options from each quadrant. There are many other forms to be discovered. These are the *building blocks* on which to build future ideas.

Ideas can be mixed and matched when designing a spindle. This means that parallel and twisted axes as well as circular and arc type outcomes can be combined on one spindle.

Quadrant 1: Arc Types, Parallel Axes

This quadrant is composed of spindles that have two things in common: parallel axes and cuts that intersect creating arc type spindles.

Both spindles are turned on two parallel axes that are 180 degrees apart or in the same plane with and equidistant from the center axis. In the left-hand photo, the profile is a bead, a cove, and a bead on one parallel axis and a cove, a bead and a cove on the other parallel axis. In the right-hand photo, the cut is deeper at one end and shallower at the other end. These axes are parallel even though they look like the axis was twisted, due to the cut being deeper at one end than the other.

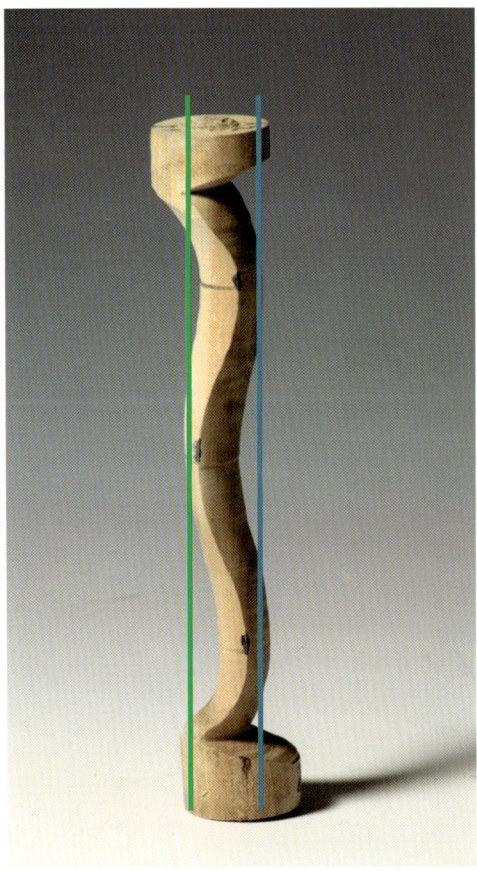
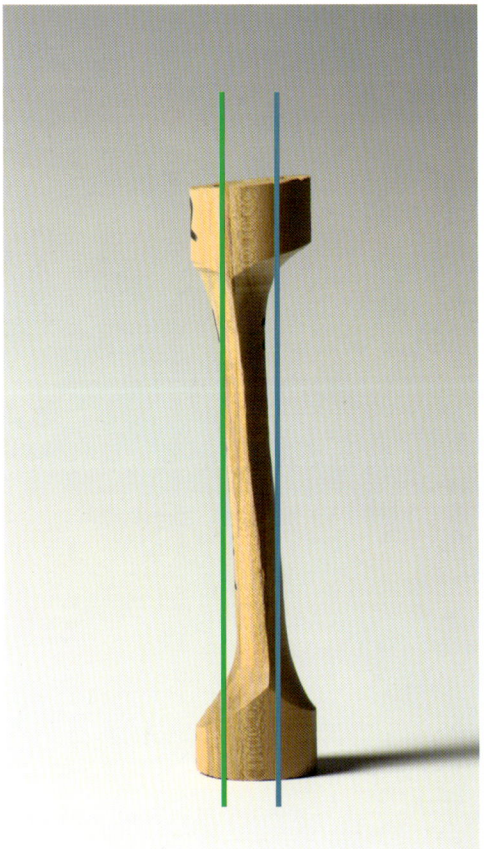

These two spindles are examples of parallel axes that are 90 degrees apart. In the left-hand photo, the axes in each segment are in the same plane with and equidistant from the center axis. Every other segment is 90 degrees apart. Below is a drawing that shows how the axes are arranged.

In the right-hand photo, the top half is turned on two axes that are in the same plane with and equidistant from the center axis. The bottom is turned on axes that are in the same plane with and equidistant from the center axis and are 90 degrees from the top part. The profile turned on both the top section and the bottom section is a cove on one axis and a bead on the opposing axis.

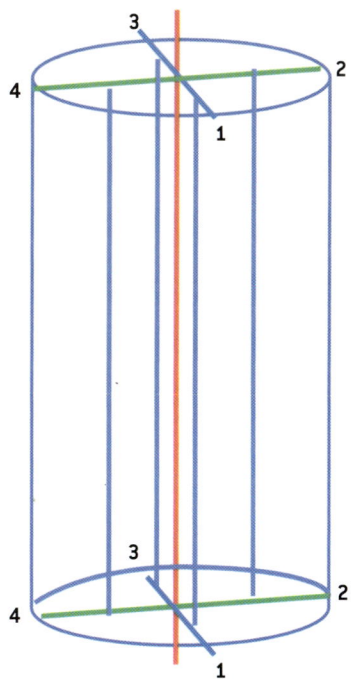

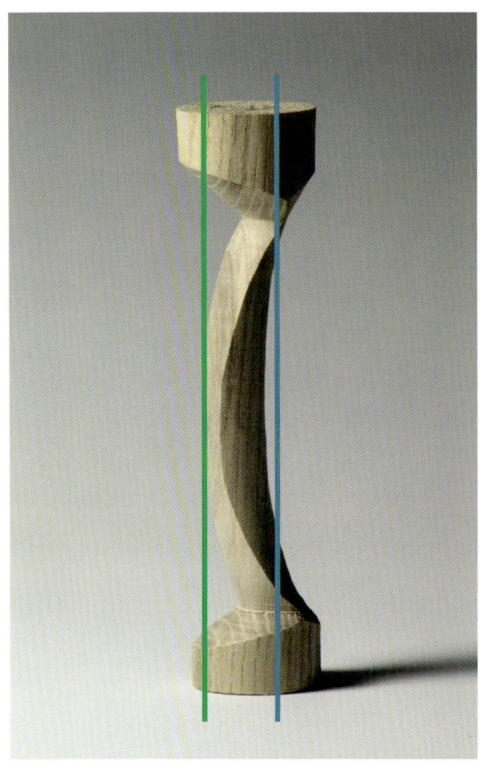

In this group of spindles, all are turned on parallel axes and all have coves, beads, and/or v-cuts as the profile in various positions. The above spindles are turned on parallel axes that are in the same plane as the center axis. The left-hand spindle has a cove on the green axis and a bead on the blue axis. The right-hand spindle has a bead, a cove, and a bead that are turned along the blue axis and the cove, a bead and a cove are turned on the green axis.

The spindle at right has three parallel axes that are separated by 120 degrees. Symmetrical coves are turned on each side.

All of these spindles have two parallel axes that are in the same plane and equidistant from the center axis. Spindle **1** has two parallel axes that are 180 degrees apart. Short coves are turned on each axis and the coves are opposite from each other. Spindle **2** is the same but with alternating coves. Spindle **3** is the same but with alternating beads. Spindle **4** is the same but with alternating v-cuts. If the v-cuts were cut deeply enough, this would become a circular type of spindle. *These are all examples of the experimentation that creates building blocks for future designs.*

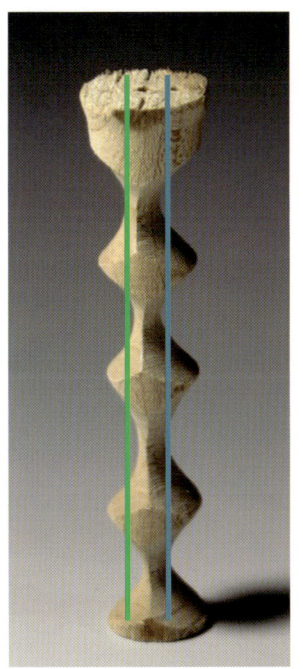

1. Opposite coves

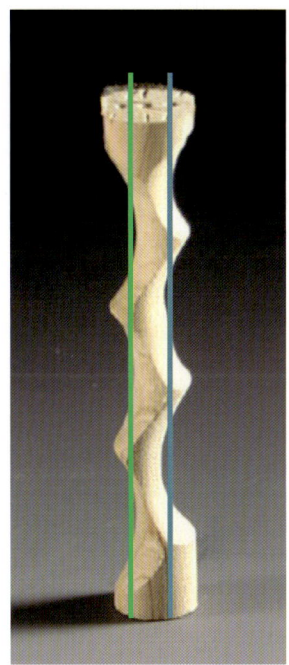

2. Alternating coves

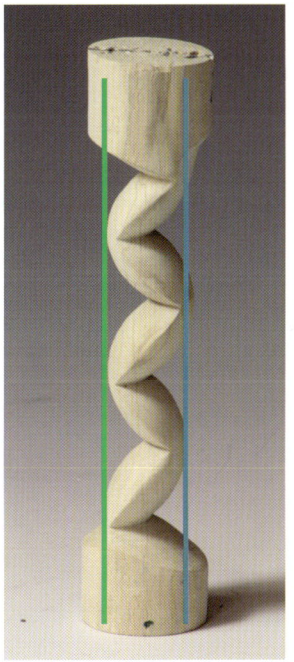

3. Alternating beads

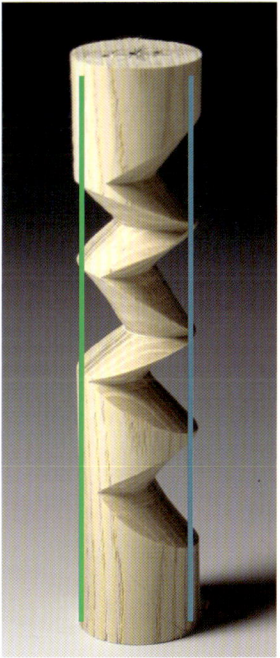

4. Alternating v-cuts

Quadrant 2: Arc Type, Twisted Axes

This quadrant is composed of spindles that have two things in common: nonparallel or twisted axes and profiles that intersect creating arc type spindles. The spindle below has two axes that are twisted by ninety degrees. A long cove is turned on each side. The drawing illustrates this twist. A long cove is turned on each axis, creating the visual twist.

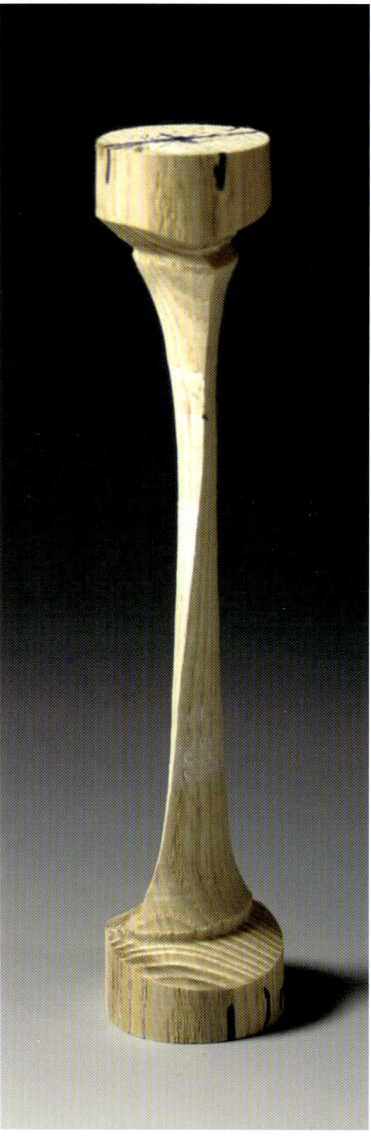
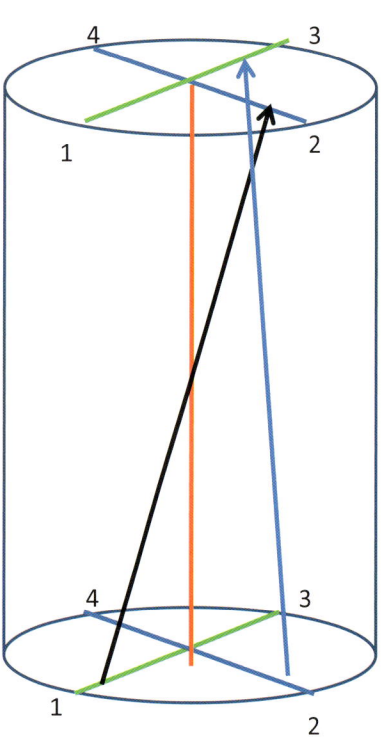

The below spindle has three axes that are separated by 120 degrees and the twist is 120 degrees. Coves are turned on each side. The drawing lllustrates this twist. These axes are all the same distance from the outside of the spindle, although they don't have to be, as there are no rules regarding axis placement.

Many other experiments can be tried here. The axes can be placed any distance from the center axis; the twist can be a random twist of, say, sixty-six degrees or forty-eight degrees. Many other profiles can be played with. Once again, these are merely *building blocks* on which future work can be made.

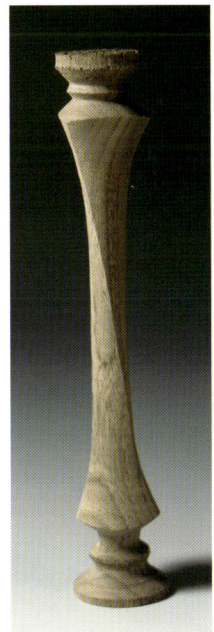
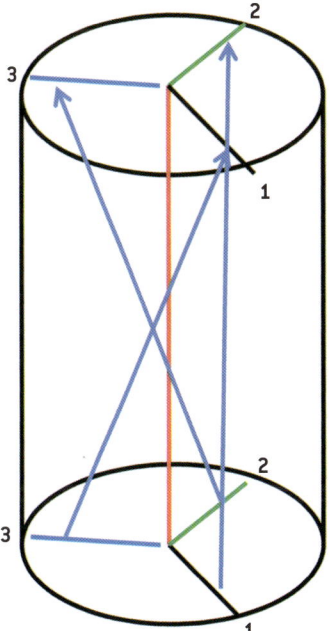

This three-sided vessel is made by Charles Brooks, who did a demo at SWAT (Southwestern Association of Turners, Texas) in 2012. The axes are 120 degrees apart and the twist is probably fifteen degrees. This demonstrates that the degree of the twist is an important element of the design.

I saw that using two axes when making a 180-degree twist ended up as a circle in the middle where the axes intersected (photo at left). So I moved on and did not think much about this twist. But soon after, woodturners Charlie Belden, Peter Rand, and I started communicating.

This twist intrigued us. The three of us shared many e-mails through the years discussing various aspects of multi-axis turnings.

Peter found some wonderful forms while playing with the idea of making an arc type twist that would *approach* 180 degrees using two axes. Below are Peter Rand's "foundlings" as seen on WOW (World of Woodturners) in March 2012. Notice that the size of the wood is wider and that he used different profiles on each axis.

During those exchanges among the three of us, Peter, who is a research scientist, explained this by using a mathematical equation, Charlie used the software SketchUp to explain this, and I used drawings based on mathematical logic. This is important because it shows how many ways there are to think about and explain phenomena.

This drawing represents the way I visualize a twist on two axes that approaches 180 degrees. Note that the blue axis intersects the black diameter on top and the blue diameter on the bottom, placing it a few degrees behind the green axis. The green axis intersects the black diameter on the top and the blue diameter on the bottom.

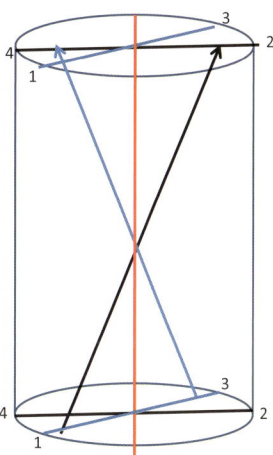

Quadrant 3: Circular Type, Parallel Axes

This quadrant is composed of spindles that have two things in common: parallel axes and cuts that go through the air wood to the solid wood and create a cylinder, creating circular type spindles. These are some of the examples that I found in this family of spindles. Initially I found *few* forms in the quadrant that I thought were interesting.

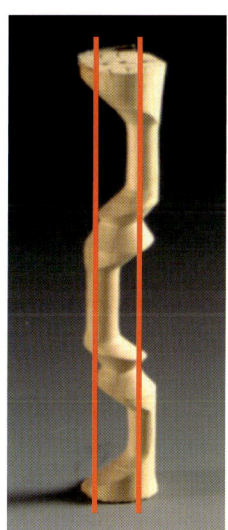

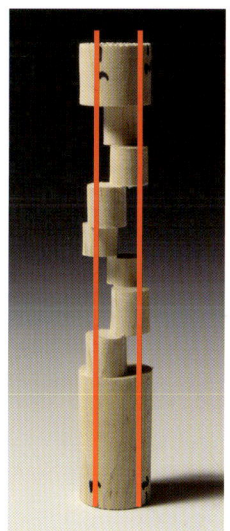

This spindle is made on two axes. A cut is made through the air wood and a cylinder is turned on each axis. The red lines show just some of the axes used.

This spindle is made on four parallel axes. The axes are rotated in sequence and a cylinder is made on each new axis. This illustrates how critical it is to have the new axes closer to the center axis. Otherwise, there would be little to no wood to connect each axis.

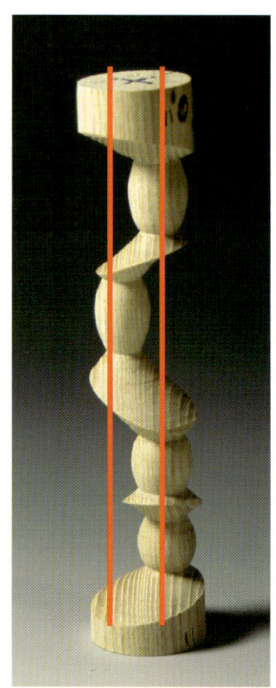

This spindle is turned on three parallel axes. A v-cut was made on each end to define the first axis. The bead was turned on the top axis; a v-cut was made to define the second axis on each end of the other two axes. A variety of beads were turned on the new cylinder on each axis.

When teaching in New York several years ago, I met Jerry Alonzo. He brought in this photo and said that he had made this sculpture while at Anderson Ranch Arts Center many years ago and did not remember how he had done it. He was a family judge, and the sculpture represented a judge and a family of three. It is a fabulous example of spindles made in quadrant three, circular type with parallel axes. Notice that the size and shape of the wood makes a huge difference in the design of a sculpture. He also used the surfaces for a canvas on which to texture and color. His work made me appreciate the ideas that are found in this family of spindles.

Quadrant 4: Circular Type, Twisted Axes

This quadrant is composed of spindles that have two things in common: nonparallel or twisted axes and cuts that go into the new solid wood of the new axis creating a cylinder. Most of the multi-axis turning that I had made in using the random "hit or miss" method fell into this quadrant. At that time, I was randomly changing the axis and then capturing the new solid wood on which I turned a profile. Knowing the things I now know, I have many other options to explore.

These are a few examples of spindles found in this quadrant. Each of these spindles is turned on axes that have been made by moving one or both ends to create a twisted axis. A cut is made on each axis through the air wood to the solid wood. A profile is then turned on the solid wood.

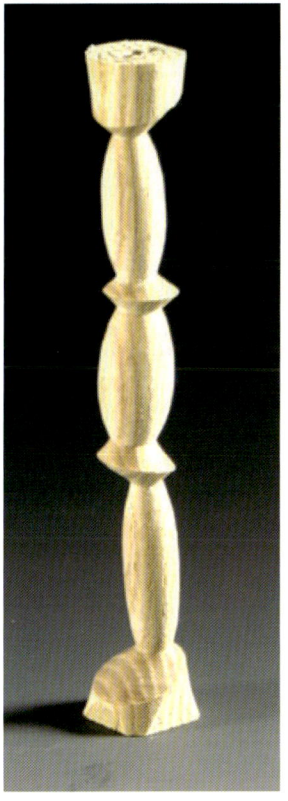

These two spindles illustrate the same idea. The first is turned on four parallel axes separated by ninety degrees. The one at far right is turned on twisted axes, one point on one end and four points on the other end. The axes are drawn on the image and show that the twisted axes were made by moving only one end and using the center point on the top end.

This shows how ideas from each quadrant can be experimented with in other quadrants.

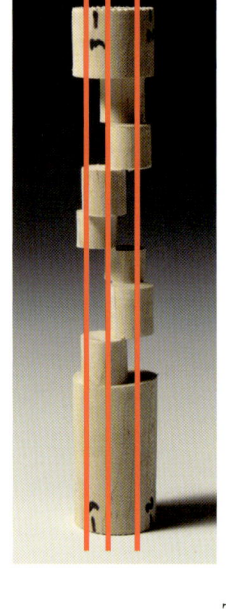
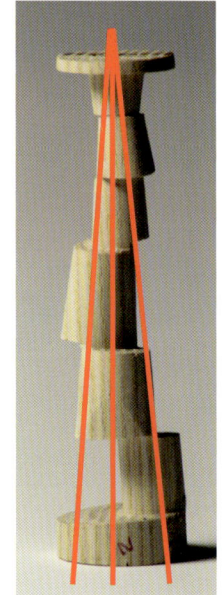

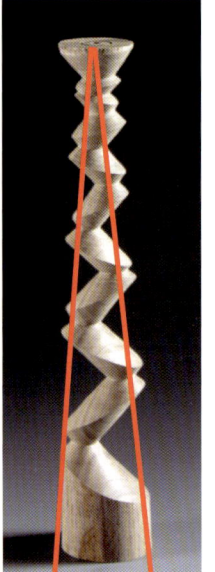

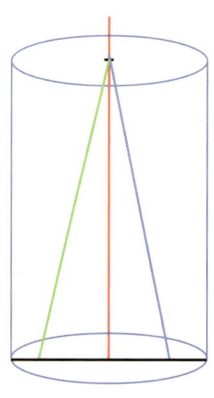

The two pieces at left are also made by changing the axes on only one end. The axes on the bottom are separated by 180 degrees. These wide v-cuts are made through the air wood and at the bottom of each v-cut is the circular part.

Examples Showing Combinations of These Ideas

This spindle is an example of combining a circular and arc type on one spindle. The top section has three axes that are parallel. The bead was turned on the center axis. The bottom section has three twisted axes. The three axes are separated by 120 degrees.

The first multi-axis goblets that I made are shown above. They were made by turning the cup, the stem, and the base separately and then attaching the three parts. I had made hundreds of experimental spindles and wanted to find a way to use them. The cups and the bases are both turned on one axis. The stems are both arc and circular types and have both parallel and twisted axes.

In April of 2012, Marshal Gorrow posted a YouTube video made by Antti Sorvama on World of Woodturning or WOW. I saw that he had turned the cup and left most of the wood below it. This gave more wood to create an interesting stem for the goblets. I have yet to explore the limits of the size of wood that can be used and the limits of the speed of the lathe.

The below group of goblets is an example of objects that have multiple axes that converge on one end (one point on one end and multiple points on the other end). Both arc type and circular type can be made this way. They were turned from one piece of wood.

After the cup is formed and hollowed, the tenon is used to offset the spindle and create the twisted axes. The four-jaw chuck is loosened and the tenon is pulled out a bit on a side and then the jaws are tightened. The wood underneath the cup is not thinned out, leaving more wood to create more interesting profiles.

Here are three goblets that have been made by moving the tenon in the four-jaw chuck. On the left is one I had made years before and is the only one I made then, as I was unimpressed with my result. I had removed too much of the wood on the stem before I twisted the axes and my outcome was less than remarkable. The one in the center is a circular type. It is made by marking 90 degrees on the base and twisting the spindle in sequence so that the axes swirl. The one on the right is an arc type and is twisted on three axes.

This drawing shows how the axes are when the tenon is used on one end. The end that is in the four-jaw chuck hardly moves. Many axes can be used on the other end.

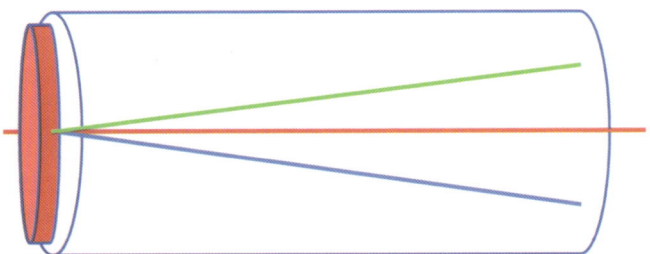

In this set of small goblets, 120-degree axes are marked and the spindle is moved to each axis in sequence so that the axes swirl.

Variations on a Theme

The arc type twisted spindle with three axes symmetrically placed at 120 degrees apart, as in the example at below left, is an idea that can be made using various sizes of wood and various degrees of twist from the top to the bottom and symmetrical or asymmetrical profiles.

I made many goblets with this as the stem. I then noticed that I could make the cup and the base on three axes as well as the stem (below right).

Then came the fun of making other items using this same concept and varying the shape and size of the wood and the symmetry of the coves.

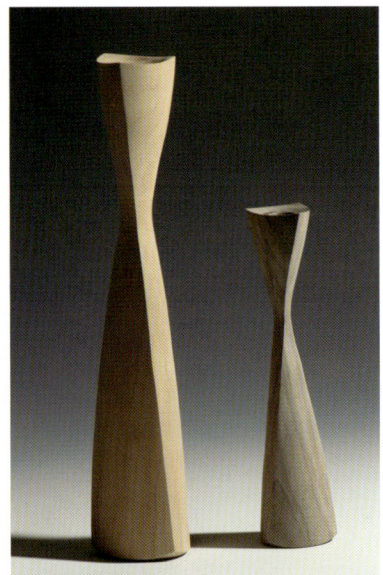

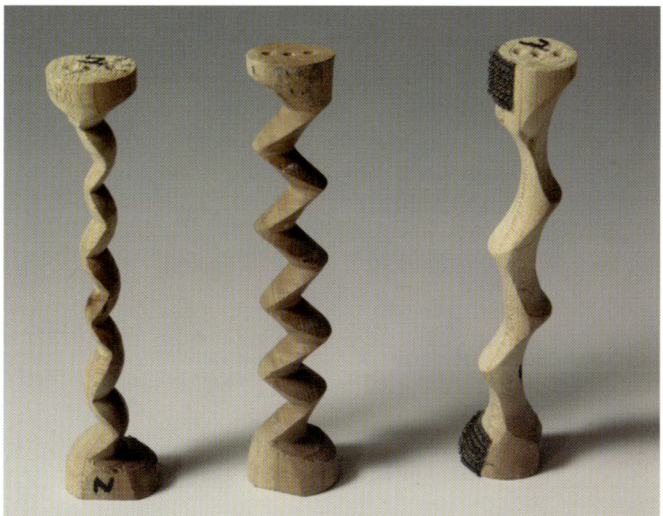

These small spindles are a few of the many that I made as I was brainstorming ideas that came from understanding how axes and outcomes were related. These are alternating beads, coves, and v-cuts on parallel axes and they eventually became the basis for a larger body of work for me.

Years later, I took these small ideas and played with them using more than two parallel axes. The spindle on the left has two parallel axes; the one in the middle has three, and the one on the right has four. All have alternating beads.

Then I wondered what would happen if I used twisted axes. The one on the left is alternating beads; the one in the middle is alternating v-cuts and the one on the right is alternating coves, all on three twisted axes. Notice that alternating v-cuts and coves, if measured accurately, create a screw.

This trio is the result of playing with simple ideas such as alternating beads or coves or v-cuts. The tall walnut sculpture on the left is from a split turning. (See chapter six.)

3

THE BASICS OF THE VARIABLES

This chapter can be used as a reference chapter as it contains the basic ideas of the variables as well as more complex realities. *All of these variables apply to every spindle in each quadrant or family.*

There are many variables such as axis placement, profile, symmetry of profile, size and shape of the wood, orientation of the cut to the center axis . . . and on. As you can see, this can all become quite confusing. I find it helpful to organize some of the variables so that I can more readily find them when considering how to approach a spindle. Visualize a spindle on one axis and then dissect it. Dissecting a one axis spindle into the three primary elements makes it easier to remember the variables that can be used on the many other axes.

The Anatomy of a Spindle on One Axis

When you dissect a simple one-axis spindle, it is clear that there are three distinct elements. The three essential elements of a spindle are the axes used, the profile, and the size and shape of the wood.

Profile:

The basic elements include:
• the cove;
• the bead;
• the v-cut;
• the straight line.

Each element can be either symmetrical or asymmetrical.

Axes:

The new axes can differ in:
• being closer to the outside of the spindle or closer to the center of the spindle;
• different axes can be used on each segment;
• the number of points used on each end;
• the angle that separates the axes (on the ends) and
• if the angle between the axes is symmetrical or asymmetrical;
• the angle of rotation from one end to the other end;
• the plane the axes are in in relation to the center axis;
• the way the axes are connected, i.e., the transition points;
• the axis used to resolve or end the spindle on each end.

The size and the shape of the wood:

When the same idea that is turned on a long and slender piece of wood is then turned on a short and wider piece of wood, the design is totally changed.

The combinations of the variables, in addition to the four basic families, offer endless possibilities for spindles that are very different.

Axis Placement

Even though there are two basic ways to place a new axis (parallel or nonparallel relative to the center axis), there are limitless options. The following diagrams outline a few ideas.

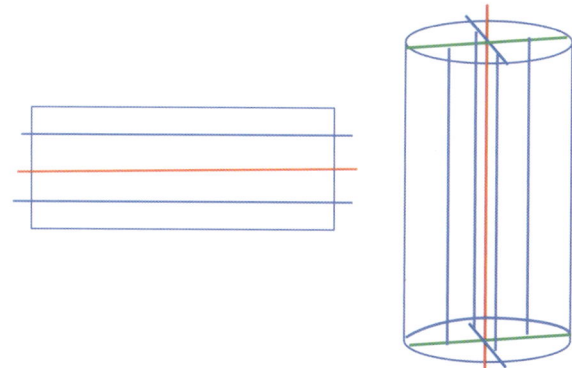

Any number of parallel axes can be used to create a form. These axes can be placed any direction and any distance from the center axis as long as each end is moved the same distance and direction from the center axis (see drawings above). Any number of axes can be used. They can be separated by equal degrees or by random degrees.

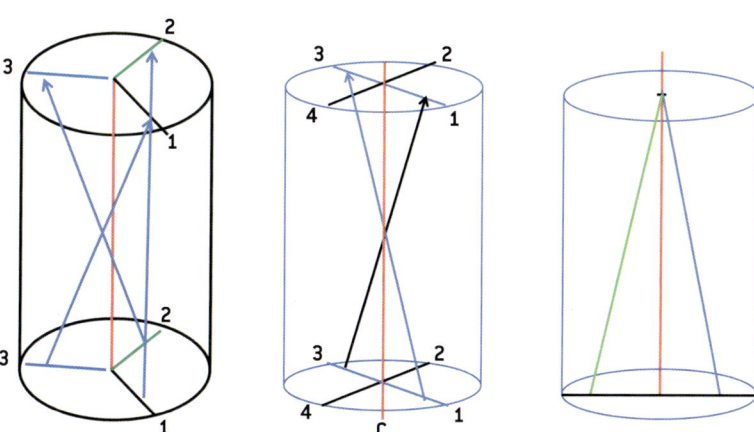

A *twisted* axis exists when one or both ends are moved in a different direction and distance from the center axis so that the new axis intersects (at some point) the center axis or a line parallel to the center axis. Any number of axes can be used.

The axes can be separated symmetrically or asymmetrically. The numbers of points on each end can vary.

The angle of an axis as it crosses through the spindle wood can be made very large by using the sides of the wood rather than the ends (right).

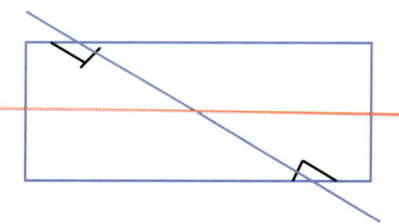

In the book *Multi-Centre Woodturning*, Ray Hopper freely uses axes placed anywhere that allow him to turn objects like a seal with a ball on his nose and other interesting projects. He also uses sizes and shapes of wood to make objects like bananas. Seeing his work and his drawings made a big impact on me.

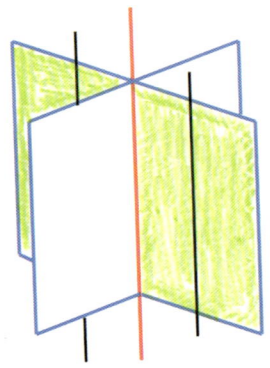

The axes drawn on the green plane are in the same plane as the center axis.

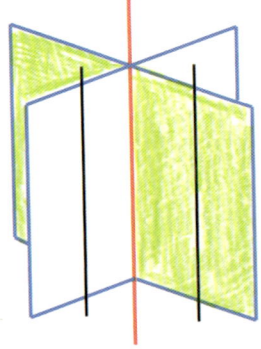

Here, the axes are in different planes that are 90 degrees apart relative to the center axis.

Most of the forms that are discussed here have less extreme angles and the new axes are placed on the ends of the spindles rather than the sides.

Since the center axis is referenced when identifying parallel or twisted axes, it can also be referenced when describing where the new axes are located. When describing two axes that are in the same plane *as the center axis*, they are, by definition, 180 degrees apart. A way to describe axes that are *not* in the same plane as the center axis is to tell the degrees of separation from each other and how close they are from the center or the outside of the spindle.

Having a vocabulary to describe where the axes are placed is a critical part of communicating to others details about a process.

Axis Placement and Its Relationship to the Circular Type Spindle

The radius of a *cylinder* is the distance from the point of the new axis to the *outside* of the spindle. The distance of the new axis from the outside of the spindle is a factor that determines the amount of solid wood that is available. When creating a cylinder on a twisted axis, the length of the radius changes at any point along the length of the spindle.

These drawings show how the placement of the new axis defines the maximum amount of solid wood in a circular type *twisted* spindle. Here, each end of the new axis is moved the same distance from the center axis and is in the same plane. Note that there is more solid wood in the center of the spindle than there is at each end, where the new axis is closer to the outside of the spindle.

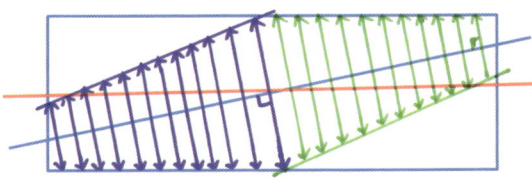

This drawing shows the placement of the new axis. The lines represent the radii from the axis to the outside of the spindle. This defines the solid wood available.

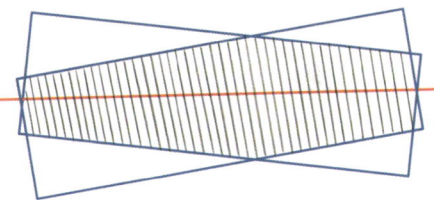

This drawing shows how the spindle looks as it spins on the new axis. The shaded wood represents the new solid wood found on that axis. The red line is the original center axis of the spindle.

In the below example, the center point is used on the right end and a point closer to the outside of the spindle is used on the left end. This clearly shows that there is more solid wood when the axis is closer to the center axis and less solid wood when the axis is closer to the outside of the spindle.

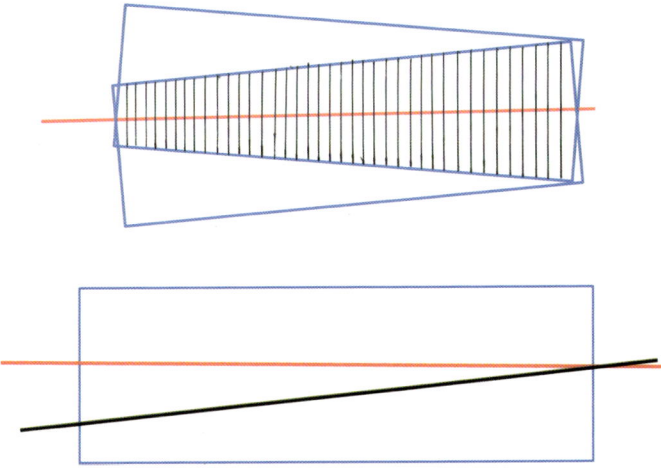

When creating a circular type on a *parallel* axis, the length of the radius is the same at any point on the length of the spindle. When the new axis is closer to the outside of the spindle, the new solid wood is less than the solid wood made when the new axis is placed closer to the center of the spindle.

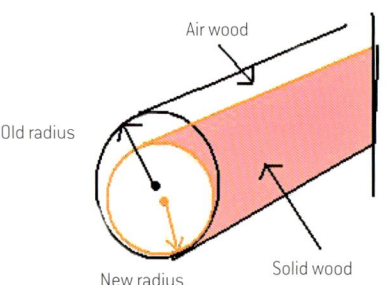
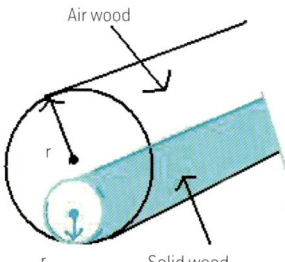

In general, the new axis should be closer to the center of the spindle when turning a circular outcome to ensure that there is enough wood to allow the axes to connect and to provide enough wood on which to turn a profile.

The Length of the Radius and How It Applies to Arc Type

The radius of an arc type spindle is the distance from the point of the new axis to the profile being cut in the *air wood*. When making an arc type outcome, the length of the radius determines the curve or arc of the cut and therefore impacts the resulting thickness of the spindle.

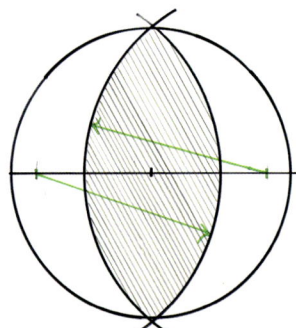
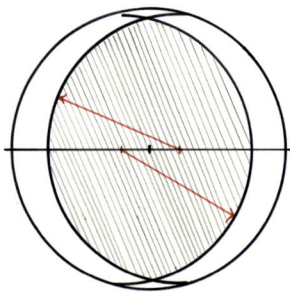

A longer radius (a radius closer to the outside of the spindle) will create an arc that is flatter.

Conversely, a shorter radius (a radius closer to the center of the spindle) creates a more rounded arc.

Transition Points between Segments Turned on Each Axis

There are many ways to connect the axes. On a circular type, one strategy is to cut through the air wood using a v-cut to define the segment. Each segment is then connected with a disc.

It took a while for me to discover that there are many ways to connect the axes. Decades ago, my strategy was to turn a profile, then switch the axis, and if I cut a v-cut when making each axis, a disc would appear. The red lines show the v-cuts taken through the air wood to the solid wood. The circular elements are turned on the newly formed cylinder.

Here are some other options. V-cuts can be made on the center axis and then each axis can be turned using ideas found in any quadrant.

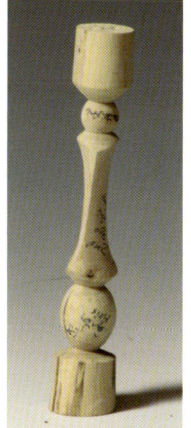

A bead can be turned on a center axis and then any idea found in any quadrant can be used on each end.

Jean-François Escoulen uses a half bead connected to a cove on many of his turnings. The pieces shown at left were turned by John Pirson.

I watched a demonstration by Michael Hosaluk and saw that he sometimes used wider pieces of wood and connected each axis differently. On these spindles, the v-cut was turned first through the air wood to define the circular outcome. (See the red arrows.) Half beads are turned on each side. Each axis intersects on the edges of the half bead. (See the green arrows.)

I played with this idea and found that it is more successful on wider pieces of wood. The two candleholders on each side are more dramatic than the tall one in the middle.

Connecting the Spindle to a Project

I used to always return to the original center axis to complete a turning. I never thought about using another axis for the final axis. After I took a sculpture class, I began to experiment with making objects that seemed to interact with each other. I then discovered that any axis can be used to connect the spindle to a project, even axes that were not used to make the spindle.

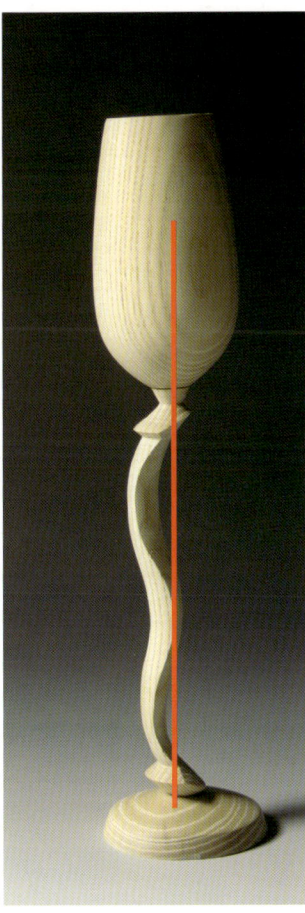
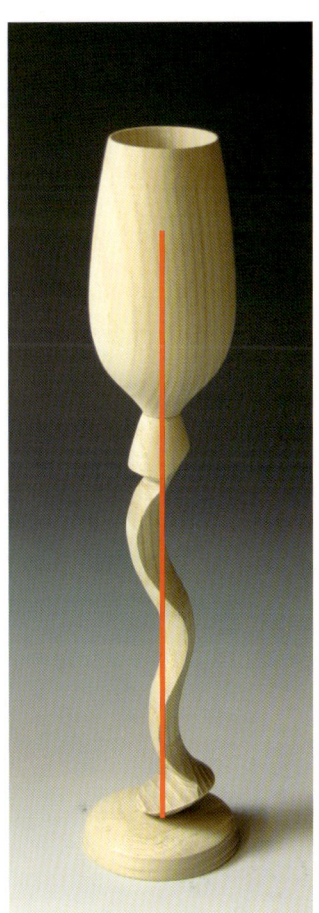

Center axis   Parallel axis   Twisted axis

These goblets show the results of using a different axis to connect the spindle to the cup and the base. Each spindle on the goblets was turned on two parallel axes which were in the same plane. However, the final axis used has a design impact on the goblet. The original center axis was used on the left-hand goblet. On the center goblet, a parallel axis was used. This is one of the axes used to create the spindle. On the goblet at right, a twisted axis was used. This axis was not used to create the spindle. The red lines show the axis used to connect the spindle to the cup and stem.

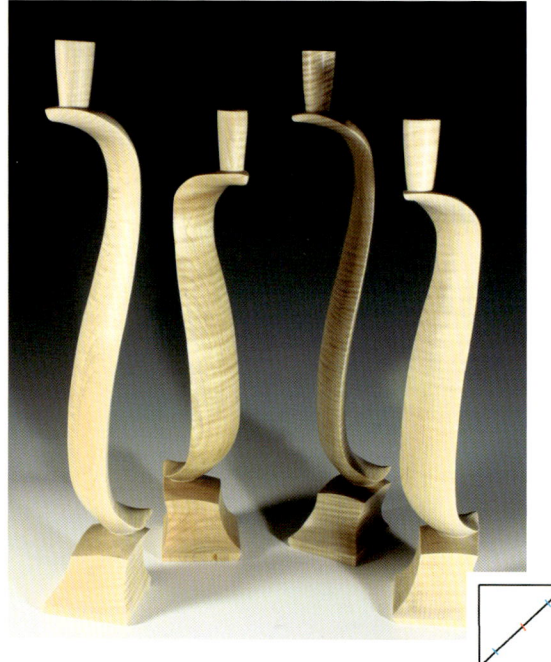

These four candleholders are a product of a split turning. (Split turnings are a way to make larger multi-axis forms, since the turning is balanced. Four large pieces of wood were glued together to turn the profile on two sides of the spindles. More information about split turnings is found in chapter four.) I mention them here because of the design element made by the axes used to finish the design after they were turned together.

The top section and the bottom section have different axes. They are placed on the diagonal and not in the center of each spindle. The split turnings have parallel axes and are arc type, as are *all* split turnings. The top and the bottom sections also have parallel axes and are circular. These candleholders are about twenty-two inches tall and three inches square.

The goblet at right is an example of finishing a split turning on the center axis of the spindle.

Basics of the Profile

The profile can be broken down to these simple elements: a bead, a cove, a v-cut and a straight line.

Each of these elements can be either symmetrical or asymmetrical. Each element or part of an element can be turned in any sequence to create the desired design. All of the many architectural spindles that exist are a product of turning a profile on a piece of wood that can vary in size and that has *one* axis. Imagine, now, how moving an axis and/or adding some axes adds an infinite number of variations that can now be discovered.

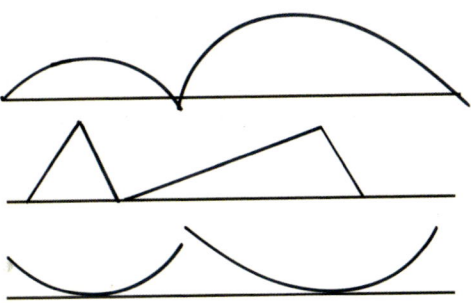

This drawing illustrates both symmetrical and asymmetrical elements of the profile.

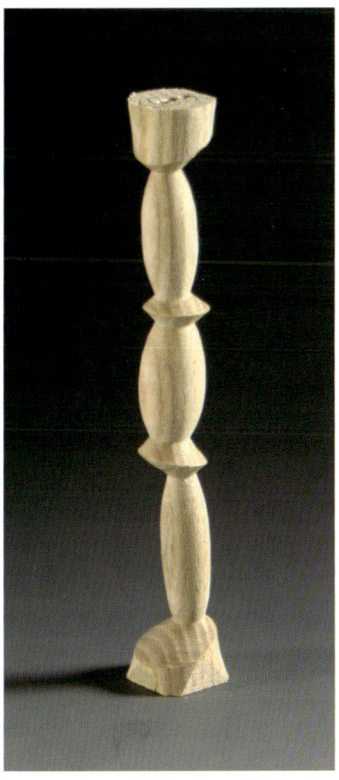

Symmetrical beads on circular type

Asymmetrical cove and bead on arc type

65

Depth of Cut

The most critical issues regarding the depth of cut are 1) will there be enough wood left after changing the axes and 2) the design elements.

Nothing trumps playful experimentation on a specific idea to understand what the depth of cut should be on that project. Each spindle that is turned teaches many important concepts. These three spindles all have three axes that are 120 degrees apart and the same distance from the center axis. The spindle on the left is thicker, as the depth of cut was minimal. The spindles in the middle and on the right were cut more deeply than the one on the left.

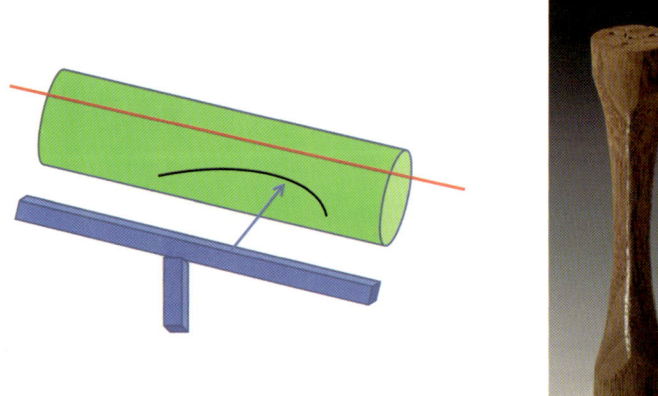

"How do you know how deep to make the cut?" is a very common question. This question reminds me of one particular question I had when I began turning. "How do you know what is inside the log so you can make the best cut when making a bowl blank?" Over time, one learns how to predict the best cut for that wood. It's not always the best cut, because you never really know until the log is opened. There are tricks to be discovered and many design opportunities to be found.

When turning coves on arc type *parallel* axes, decide how thin you want the thinnest part of the spindle to be. The tool rest can be used as a fixed point to measure the distance to the desired depth on all sides if your tool rest is long enough and will not be moved.

When turning coves on arc type *twisted* axes, one trick is to use a parting tool to create a cylinder on the center axis that represents the desired depth of the finished cuts (plus a bit). Then each axis is turned using the cylinder as a reference depth. Another strategy is to measure the depth of the first axis and turn the other axes to that depth.

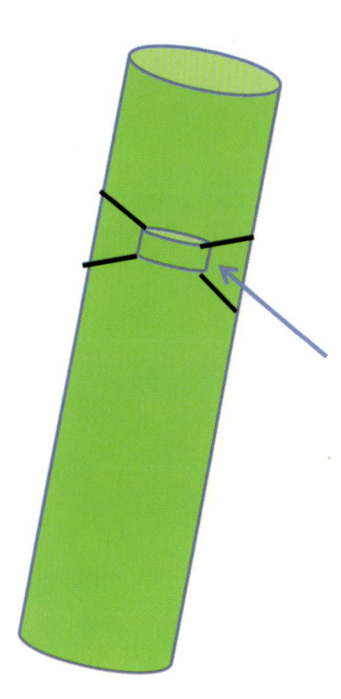

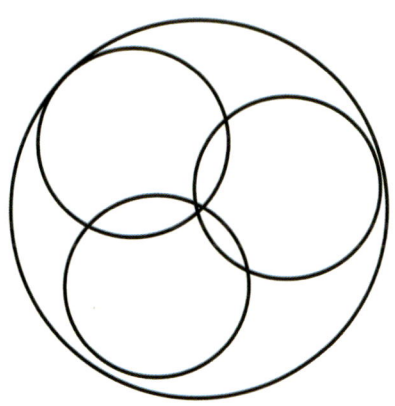

New axes closer to center

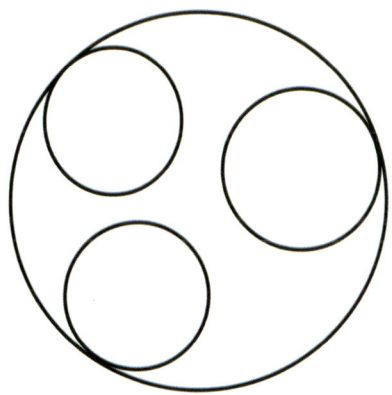

New axes closer to the outside

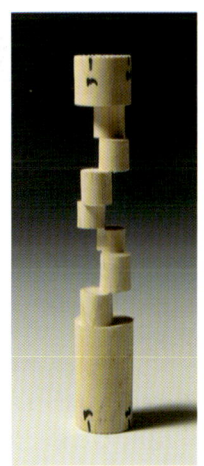

When turning circular type spindles, make sure that each new axis is closer to the center axis. This insures that there will be enough wood to not only create a new cylinder, but there will be enough wood to connect the axes. The spindle in the photo above is an example of four parallel axes with cylinders turned on each axis. If the axes had been placed closer to the outside of the spindle, each axis would not connect and it would have broken.

The Size, Shape, and Orientation of the Wood

The size and shape of the wood has an enormous impact on the design. These two pieces demonstrate how the shape and size of the wood can dramatically change the design. These two spindles were turned using nonparallel axes in the same plane with the center axis. A diameter is scribed on each end. These lines are parallel to each other. Then seven axes are marked and numbered the same on each end. Holes were pressed into each twisted axis starting with one to seven; then two to six and so on. The reason that the two spindles look like very different designs is the difference of the size and shape of the wood used to create each spindle. On a shorter and wider piece of wood, the angles are much larger than on the taller and thinner piece.

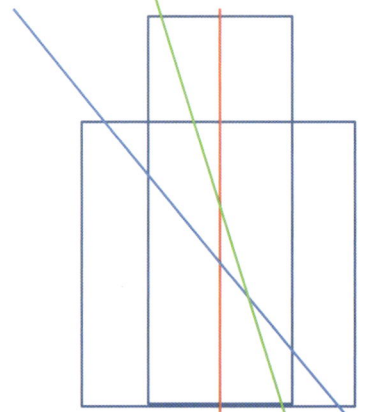
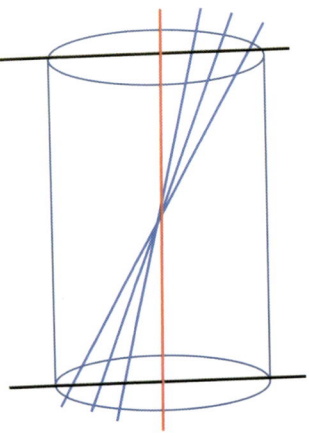

These two pieces also demonstrate how the shape and size of the wood can dramatically change the design. The one on the left was made before I understood how to think about multi-axis spindles. It was a lucky discovery. It fits into the fourth quadrant because each axis is not parallel to the center axis or any line parallel to the center axis and it is a circular type. I enjoyed this form and made a series of candleholders that had one or all elements in the design.

In 2013, I was invited to make a piece for the American Association of Woodturners show "Harmony," for the Tampa symposium. The requirements were that each piece must fit into a six-inch cube, as well as be relevant to the title of the show. I tried various ideas and just about gave up. Then I remembered this idea and decided it would be perfect. But I had to make it on a six-inch-square piece of wood. To make this from a six-inch cube involved solving many problems. It took a month and many practice pieces to make this. (See AAW *American Woodturner*, October 2013, for an article detailing the piece's design evolution.)

Ray Hopper's book, *Multi-Centre Woodturning*, is a great reference for thinking outside of the box. He uses rectangular pieces of wood to create these sculptures. The banana is an example that I borrowed from Ray's book. The banana has three axes that are placed on a line that goes through the center of each end. These lines are parallel to each other. If they are numbered the same on each end, then turn axis one to three; then two to two; then three to one.

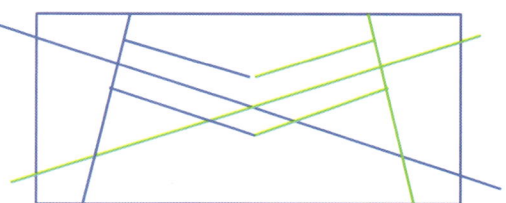

This image is a spindle turned like the banana but only two axes, one to three and three to one, are used.

It looked like a chicken leg to me, so I carved a foot and made a goblet!

Jon Siegel has written about and presented his ideas on what he calls Dutch foot legs. Multi-axis turning has been done for many years. This is one way furniture makers have used this technique. The axes are drawn on the *diagonal* and in the same plane of the center axis. This insures that the foot will face the corner rather than the side of the leg. If the line is drawn on the *diameter*, the foot would face the square edge of the spindle. Since this cannot be drawn on the wood, a way to figure out the placement of the axes is to make a full-scale drawing of the leg on paper, using the diagonal (as the width) and the length. The point at which the two axes

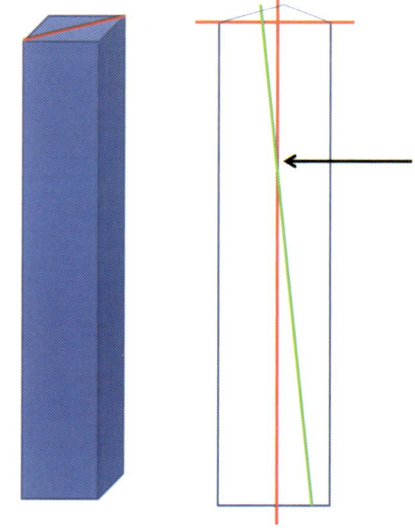

intersect is close to the top and is the point of symmetry. This is where the square turns into the rounded section. The three critical points are the placement of the axis on the top and the bottom and the point along the length that these two lines intersect. These critical points can then be transferred to the wood.

The wood is placed on the *off* axis. A cut is made where the two axes intersect near the top. A tapered cylinder is turned from the notch to the foot, and a cove connects the taper to the square at the end. The entire leg is turned on the off axis.

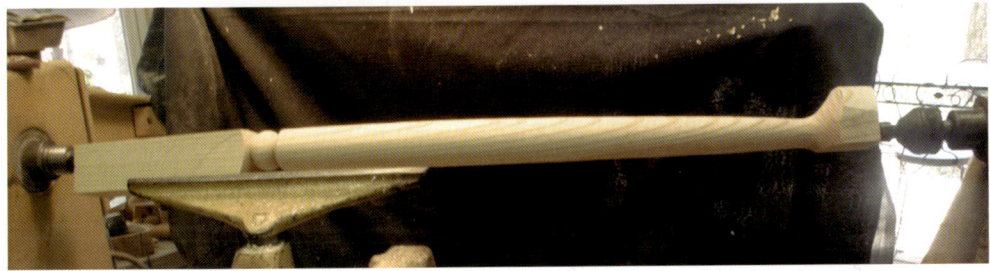

Now the wood is put onto the center axis and a half bead is turned on the bottom of the foot.

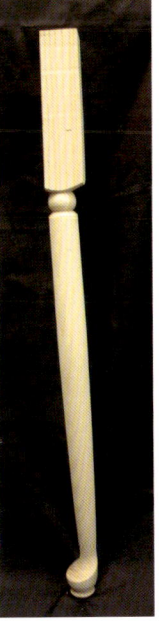

How the Length and Width of the Wood Affects a Twist

If a ninety-degree twist is turned on two axes on a short piece of wood, and if the twist is the length of the piece of wood, then the twist is ninety degrees. (See photo at right.)

This sculpture is 9" tall by 8" wide. The twist is ninety degrees from top to bottom.

If this twist is turned on a *segment* of a longer piece of wood, the actual twist is a fraction of the ninety degrees. (See photo at left.)

Knowing this means that the degree of twist can be anticipated and planned for.

This spindle is twisted ninety degrees from top to bottom. The actual twist is no more than thirty degrees, since it is a segment of the full twist.

Square...*ish* Turnings and Other Odd Orientations of the Wood

As you encounter other turned pieces in your travels, you'll find new things to incorporate into your work. I was inspired by the work of Art Liestman. I wondered if I could make something similar to his thermed pieces (see chapter four) but between centers. And when I met Luc Deroo I was fascinated with his multi-axis forms. Both turners used large rectangular pieces of wood. My work, so far, had mostly been spindle work. I decided to play with different sizes and orientations of the wood.

These are examples of forms that can be made by mounting a rectangular or square piece of wood on the lathe in very fluid ways to create just about anything.

Luc Deroo

Art Liestman

When cutting a spindle, the tool rest is usually placed parallel to the bed of the lathe. When creating square…*ish* turnings, the tool rest is anywhere from thirty degrees to ninety degrees (perpendicular) to the bed of the lathe. These cuts are similar to the cuts made when beginning a bowl and roughing out the outside of the bowl. The forms that I have made are merely concave and/or convex curves so that I can hide the offset axes that I've used.

The spout on the teapot is one of the axes used to create that surface. More wood is removed from the spout side making the tenon longer. Enough wood is removed from each side to then cut off and sand the axis that was used, making it a mystery for others to figure out how it was turned.

Short and long turnings can be created using this method of mounting and cutting the wood. When turning long and slender pieces of wood, it looks like a propeller and care must be taken to know where the wood is relative to the tool rest, the tool, and your fingers.

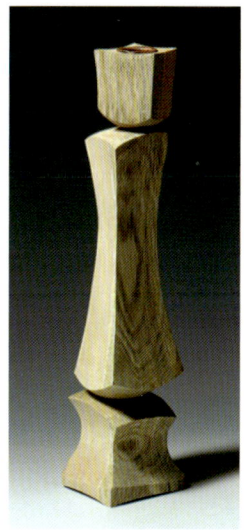

This sugar bowl is made between centers and has six sides.

The pieces on the left are made by me after seeing a demo by Derek Weidman. All of these pieces represent using a cube of wood and turning it between centers.

I have known Derek Weidman for many years. His process is fascinating and his work is fluid. Derek turns slowly. He almost has to because of the weight of the wood. He artistically places the wood on many axes to create the sculptures that he makes. He doesn't hide the points from the headstock and the tailstock. He doesn't hide the tool marks. All of these elements become important parts of his art. He burns to accent the tool marks. He uses colors. This is an example of taking an idea to another level.

Derek Weidman's work

4

SPLIT AND THERMED TURNINGS

Split and thermed turnings are both methods used to turn more than one piece of wood at the same time. These methods have the advantages of creating more than one spindle that are identical and creating balance, while allowing larger pieces of wood to be turned off center.

When turning one piece of wood on multiple axes, the weight of the wood and the placement of the new axis are both factors that create a lack of stability. Both factors potentially create varying degrees of vibration. Solutions include managing the speed and using a method of counterbalancing (see chapter six). Split and thermed turnings offer another solution for this issue.

A split turning is accomplished by attaching two or more pieces of wood together, turning them, separating them, rotating them, attaching them and turning them. The wood used is usually square or rectangular or diamond-shaped pieces that fit together. The center most often used is the center or the intersection of the pieces of wood. When the center of the intersection of the pieces is used, the result is an arc type spindle with parallel axes.

An inside out turning, or "reversal," is a split turning that has been glued back together after the sides have been turned to make a single object.

Therming is a method of turning more than one piece of wood at a time by using a jig or a waste block to hold the wood away from the axis of the lathe, thus creating flatter arcs on the sides. Each piece of wood has no contact with the axis of the lathe.

My focus has been on what happens between the headstock and the tailstock when using multiple axes on the lathe. Split turnings do fit in this exploration. I mention therming as a very interesting extension of split turning. Both techniques are a way to turn more than one piece of wood at a time using extreme axes. Both methods create balanced turnings when turning multiple pieces of wood.

Both methods result in a form that resides in the first quadrant, parallel axes and arc type, *if* the center of the glued pieces is used for split turnings and the wood placed in the therming jig is parallel to the bed of the lathe.

Thermed Turnings

For centuries, *therming* was a way to make multiples of rather square-looking pedestals. Some therming lathes had six foot swings and a jig that many pieces of wood were attached to and that created square-like pedestals. The larger diameter of the jig, the flatter the arc on the turnings, creating pedestals that appeared to be square.

Currently, several turners are using jigs to hold wood to a faceplate to create amazing off-center forms. However, few woodturners are currently using therming to turn objects. Art Liestman has used therming in his work. This teapot is one example. The wood is placed in a jig that holds the wood away from the axis of the lathe.

This is the jig that Art used to create his thermed turnings. I took these photos at Arrowmont in a class with Art. They show what the jig is like in action. See the bibliography for a useful article by Art Liestman.

Art Liestman

Art Liestman's therming jig

Split Turnings

My focus is on all things that can be made *between centers* on a lathe without using a jig. When making a split turning, two or more pieces of wood are cut to the same size and then glued and taped together. The glued-up wood is usually placed between centers in the center of each end. The drive center and the tail center do make contact with the extreme edge or corner of each piece of wood. These pieces can be triangular, square, diamond, or rectangular. A few important reasons to use this method are: 1) The lathe is balanced; therefore larger pieces of wood can be more easily turned. 2) More than one spindle is turned at a time. The result is that two to nine pieces are turned that are identical. This saves time as well as having identical spindles.

I use wood that has been cut to rectangles or squares when I use this method of turning.

When making a split turning, the wood is placed on the lathe with the turning axis in the center of the glued-up pieces of wood. This means that when turning four pieces, the extreme edge or corner of each spindle is placed between centers.

Each end forms a square or a rectangle and the axis used to turn these pieces is the center of each end. These drawings show how four squares, two rectangles and two squares of wood are attached for a split turning and where the new center axis is placed. In **A**, four pieces of wood have been cut to the same size and glued and taped together. The inside corners is the new center axis. In **B**, two rectangles have been glued and taped together. The new center axis is on the center of the edge of each piece. In **C**, two squares of spindle wood are used to make the split turning. The turning axis is on the center of the outside edge or on the extreme corner of each piece.

B and **C** differ from **A** in a very important design element. When four square pieces of wood are used for a split turning, the turning axis is on the diagonal and the profile

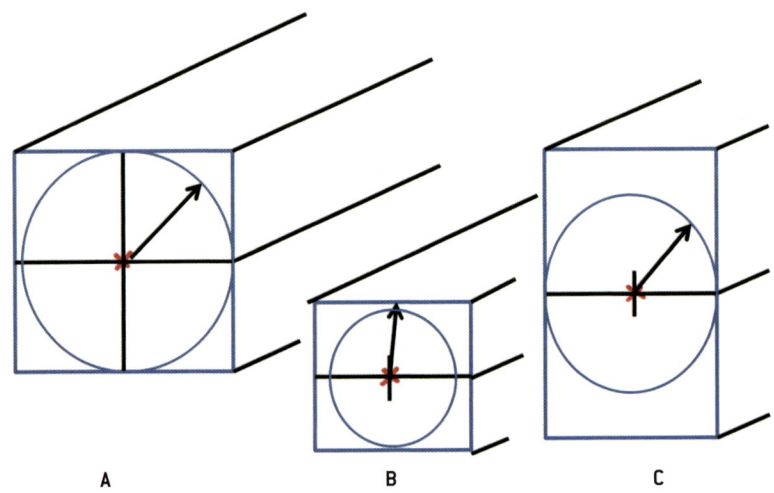

A   B   C

faces the corner of the spindle. When the new axis is on the side of the pieces of wood, as in **B** and **C**, the new axis is on the radius and the profile faces the side of the wood. When turning table legs, the axes are on the diagonal and the profile is facing the corner of the wood for this reason.

This photo shows how the length of the radius affects the diameter of the turned spindle. Split turnings demonstrate this idea perfectly, since the axes are placed on the extreme edges of the wood. The spindle on the left was made between centers and the new axes were place close to the outside of the rounded spindle. The spindle in the middle was a split turning using two pieces of wood that were about seven inches long and rectangular with one side being one inch. The axes used are on the very edge of each spindle which is on the radius of the glued-up pieces. The one on the right was a split turning using 4 pieces of wood that were 7" long and square and were glued together. The axis used was the corner of each piece which is on the diagonal of the glued-up pieces. As the radius got longer, the arc was flatter and the resulting spindle became thinner.

Depth of Cut When Turning a Split Turning with Four Squares

Knowing how deep a cut should be made is tricky. When four pieces of wood are glued together, the axes and the cut will be on the diagonal. This makes it hard to understand how deep to make the cut, as the visual is of the diagonal. On all other spindle turnings, what is visualized while turning is the radius of the spindle. This drawing shows how to think about depth of cut when turning a split turning with four squares. The red areas in this drawing show the amount of wood that is removed if the split turning is turned into a cylinder. In the upper

left square, the shaded areas show how much wood is removed if the wood is turned to a cylinder on each side. This means that if you cut deeply enough to make a cylinder on each of the four axes, then the area left in the center of this spindle would be all the wood left on which to turn a profile.

The depth of cut is more easily seen when two pieces of wood are used, since the view of the radius is seen rather than the diagonal.

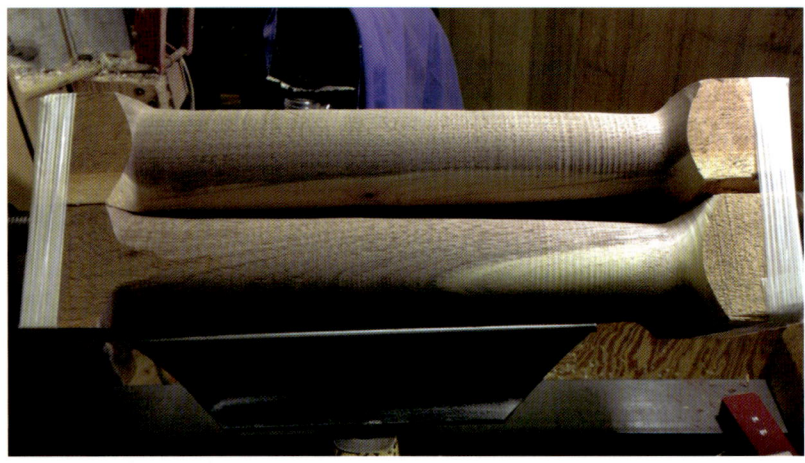

One way to solve this issue is to turn off the edges that would be turned off if only one square spindle was being turned between centers to create a cylinder.

I have not played with diamonds yet, but Peter Exton has with amazing results. While I have used squares and rectangles for my split turnings, Peter has shaped wood into long diamonds and has experimented with the relationships between the multiples that he turns. He turns three, six, or nine diamonds to create unique sculptures. See the bibliography for an article he wrote on diamonds in *American Woodturner*.

An inside out turning is a split turning that has been glued together to create a single object. Dug Campbell, a friend and fellow woodturner, is the master of the skew and the creator of some beautiful inside out turnings.

Assembling Wood for Split Turning

Prepping the wood for split turnings requires making two or four pieces of wood the exact same width and length. If the goal is to make inside out turnings or table legs, this is of utmost importance. When making objects that stand alone, the prep of the wood can be done by using a band saw rather than a table saw and jointer. This means that any wood, kiln dried or green, can be used for split turnings. I use the band saw to create straight sides and a chop saw for the ends of the wood.

Many methods have been used to attach the wood together for a split turning. Screws, hose clamps, and strong rubber bands are but a few of many methods tried. No matter what method is used, it *must* hold the wood together as it spins.

My favorite method is to use a dab of hot glue to tack the wood together and then wrap strapping tape around the pieces. I have also used Plexiglas on each end to prevent the *points* of the head and tail centers from separating the pieces of wood. I drill a hole in the Plexiglas for the points to go into. Since it is transparent, it is easy to center it. I use hot glue to secure it. This also adds another layer of security.

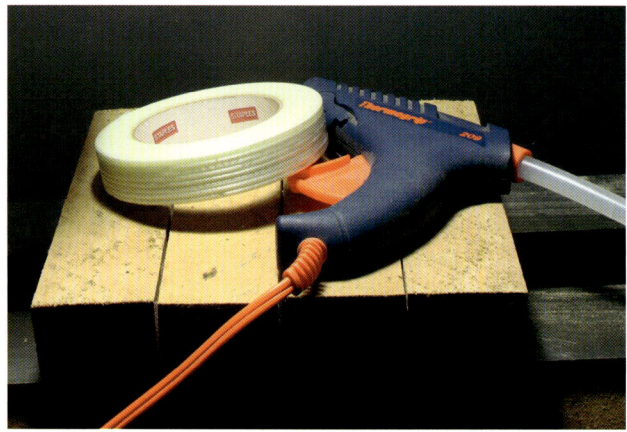

Here is a series of images that show the process in action.

There are many ways to approach making a split turning. One way is to have no concrete plan and to experiment with each side. This experimentation teaches what works and what doesn't work. Another way is to create a spindle using four parallel axes that are on the diagonal (if you are turning four squares). In the image on the right, the spindle to the left is a prototype of for split turning.

Here the squares have been glued up and Plexiglas has been glued to each end. It is then placed between centers and the ends are wrapped with strapping tape.

Next the first axis is turned. I am using a straight edge to check the depth of the cut.

I use a chisel and mallet to separate the squares of wood.

The second axis has been completed. I rotated each square ninety degrees. I sometimes rotate the squares 180 degrees.

Now all four sides have been turned.

Here they are separated and each side is facing the camera.

These two are finished. I finished one upside down.

In the image of the trio, the walnut sculpture on the left is one of the split turnings.
The other two sculptures are made with nonparallel or twisted axes.

These images are of various objects made using split turnings. The two candleholders in the left-hand photo are split turnings and were made by using four pieces of wood and rotating them on all four sides. Each was finished on the center axis of each spindle. The next two are split turnings that were rotated twice and turned on two sides. They were finished on the center axis of each spindle.

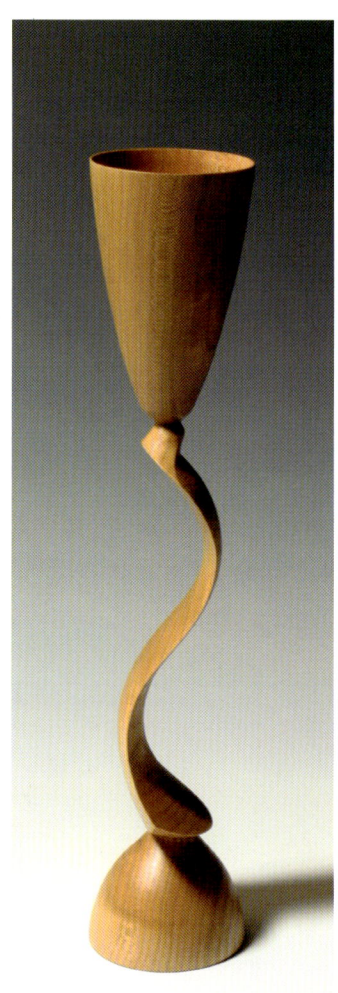

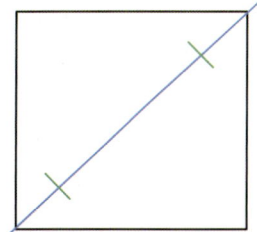

These candleholders are also split turnings. Four pieces of wood were turned and rotated only twice. They were finished by using two other parallel axes placed along the diagonal of each spindle.

5
HOW TO MAKE A THREE-SIDED CUP OR VASE

There are many projects to make using multi-axis spindle ideas. This project is one way to execute an idea and solve some of the problems that are encountered in making any object.

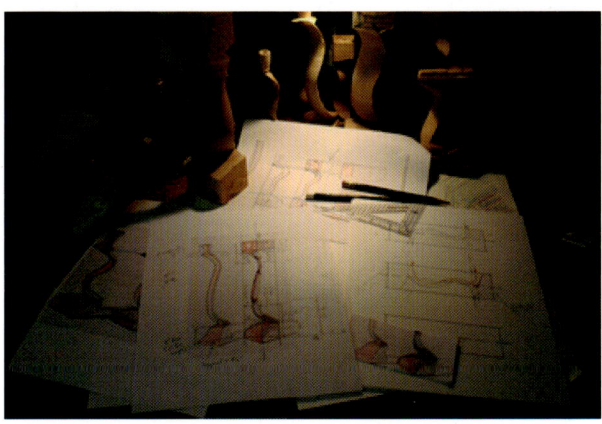

Note that most designs that are turned are *not* necessarily signature pieces. Three-sided cups are not signature pieces. They exist when three axes are used to create a cup, just as a natural edge bowl exists when the wood is turned using the bark as the rim. There are so many variables that each of us can use, such as the size of the wood, the shape of the profile, and where the axes are placed. They are fun projects that can be fun to make and to sell or give as wedding gifts.

Signature pieces *are* works that have taken thought and skill and represent the artistic voice of the maker. It may be possible to for others to understand and make a signature piece, but why copy? It will be viewed as a copy by others who know about our craft. There are an infinite number of options when basic concepts are understood.

The First Steps

So let's make a three sided object. The first thing to do is to decide what the dimensions are of the cup or vase that you want to make. To make a cup like the ones shown here, I might start with a piece of wood that is about three inches in diameter and about six to seven inches long.

How to Create Symmetry

If the goal is to make this object symmetrical, then the most problematic issue is to find a way to make each axis have the same curve and the same depth of cut.

To accomplish this, one strategy is to make a tenon on each end and put chalk on it to make it more visible. These tenons are a *guide* for the depth of the cut at the top and the bottom and have nothing to do with a four-jaw chuck yet. The tenon on the top represents the *outside* edge of the opening. So this size becomes a design element. The tenon is useful for another reason. The points used for the head and tail centers are removed when the tenons are removed. This means that the finished size of the cup is exactly as planned. If tenons are not used, some wood on each finished end would have to be removed to eliminate the points from the head and tail centers.

To create this symmetrical multi-axis cup, the axes are separated by 120 degrees and are the same distance from the center of the spindle. In this example the twist is 120 degrees.

Where to Locate the Axes?

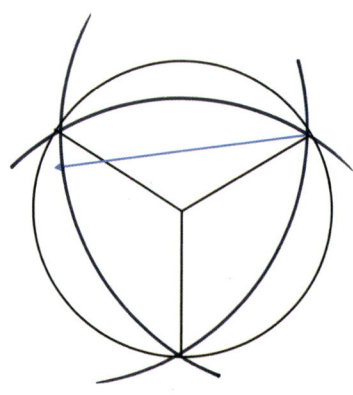

There is a way to understand where to locate the three new axes. These drawings show more details about how the placement of the axes affects the arcs that are made.

This drawing shows that when the new axes are placed on the circumference of the spindle, and when they intersect within the cylinder, the radii are longer and the arcs are flatter. The blue arrow is the new radius when the new axis is placed on or near the circumference of the spindle.

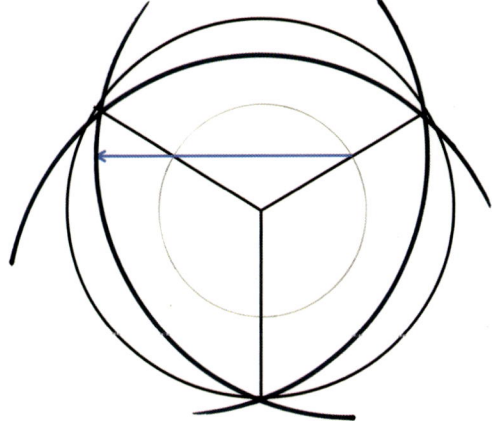 

This shows that when the new axes are placed at a point that is about one half of the radius, the arcs are a bit more curved.

In this drawing, the new axes are located closer to the center of the spindle and the arcs are more rounded. I'm sure I knew this as a young person studying math in high school, but I was surprised to see that the arc could be placed on the circumference of the cylinder and that they would intersect within the cylinder.

This means that it really doesn't matter where the new axes are located when making this project. What matters is the design element that is created with the placement of the axes. For a more rounded object, the new axes are placed close to the center axis. To create a cup that has more pronounced lines created by the intersection of each axis, the new axes are placed closer to the outside of the spindle.

How to Number the Axes

The twist can be more or less than 120 degrees. The left circle, **A**, shows a numbering system that is used religiously as long as it makes sense. This systematic way to number is simply numbering each end with the same numbers, 1-1, 2-2, and 3-3. To create a twist of 120 degrees, the axes used are 1-2, 2-3, and 3-1. The larger circle represents the headstock end and the smaller circle represents the tailstock end. I always have the lowest number on the left, or headstock end, and the next highest number on the right, or tailstock end. This twist is counterclockwise. To turn a clockwise twist, use the same numbering system but number in the opposite direction. (When I tried to calculate this mentally by reversing my system, I always got confused. So, numbering in the opposite direction is a no brainer!)

The right circle, **B**, shows an exception to the numbering system just described. In this example, the axes are separated by 120 degrees *and* the twist is forty degrees. In this situation, it is less confusing to use a different system of numbering the axes. The bottom is numbered 1, 2, and 3. The top markings are rotated to about forty degrees and are numbered 1, 2, and 3. Now the twisted axes are 1-1, 2-2, and 3-3. This is less confusing than other ways I have tried. This is but one solution to avoid confusion.

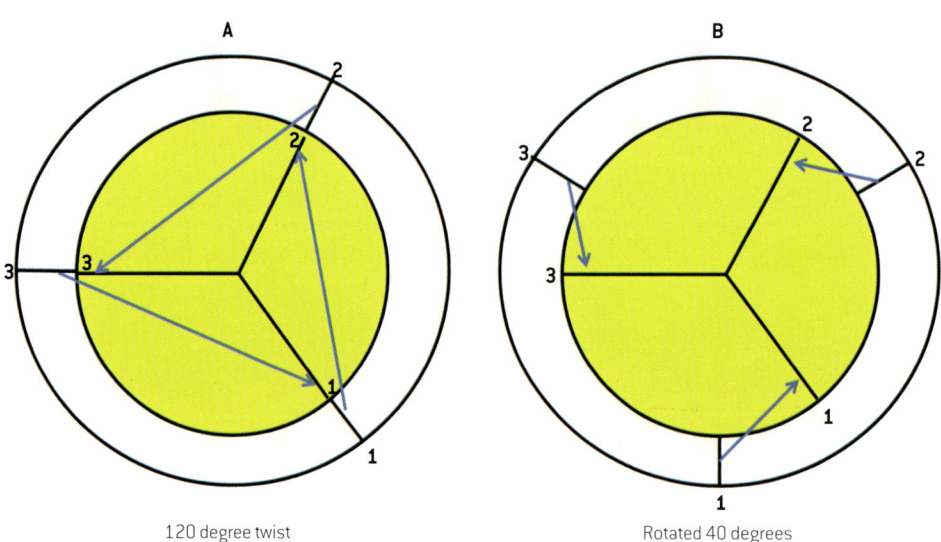

120 degree twist   Rotated 40 degrees

There are many ways to mark the angles easily. An indexing system can be used. It is simple enough to buy one or make one if the lathe does not have one.

I have also drawn concentric circles on my bench with the angles that I use the most drawn through the circles.

And I use heavy plastic from food containers to make transparent jigs with angles and concentric circles to help find not only the centers quickly, but also the angles.

Turn, Turn, Turn

Draw the points for each axis and press in the points. Turn a tenon on each end that will represent the depth of cut. Use chalk to make the tenons more visible.

Then mount the cup on the first axis. Make a cut on both ends that touches the tenon. This defines the desired depth.

Draw the points for each axis and press in the points.

Mount the cup on the first axis.

The next challenge is to match the curves on each side. The tool rest can be used as a reference point for both the depth and the narrowest part of the curve. This works if it is not moved while turning all three axes. Turning similar coves takes practice and visual memory. When turning the other axes, use the tenon as a guide for the depth of cut and then turn the curve connecting the two ends.

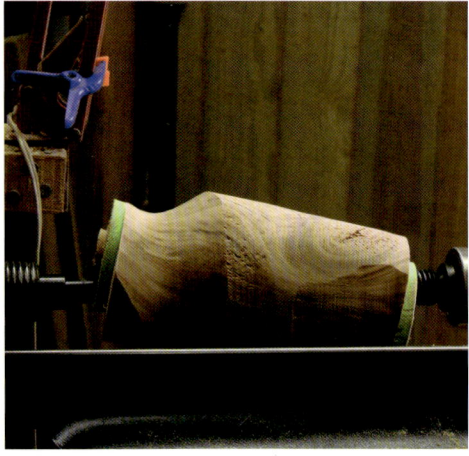

Make a cut that touches the tenons on both ends.

The first axis is finished. The cove is deeper on the bottom of the cup to make the finished cup easier to hold.

When turning the other two axes, use the tenons on each end as guides for the depth of cuts. Then turn the cove that connects the two ends.

If the curves are similar, the beautiful lines that connect the twist of the axes are smooth.

After the three axes are turned, place the spindle on the center axis. Turn the tenon on the bottom to the size needed for the four-jaw chuck. While between centers, remove the tenon on the top.

Then carefully hollow the cup. It will be thinner in some places. Sand the inside while still on the lathe. Then reverse chuck it and remove the tenon on the bottom. This is done by using a jam chuck.

I have used thin CA glue for years to seal the inside of cups and bowls. This glue comes in various thicknesses. The thin glue soaks into the cells of the wood and, when dry, becomes an inert plastic.

Summary:
Turn wood into a cylinder;
Turn tenons on each end that are used for visualizing the depth of cut;
Decide the placement of the new axes;
Color tenons with chalk for visibility;
Mark angles and number the axes;
Turn each axis using the tenons to determine the depth of the cut on each end;
Turn the desired curve;
Form the tenon for the four-jaw chuck and place between centers;
Remove the tenon on the cup end and tweak the tenon on the bottom end so it will fin into the chuck;
Hollow the inside;
Sand the inside of the cup while it's on the lathe;
Reverse chuck to remove the tenon on the bottom;
Use CA glue to finish the inside (this dries into an inert plastic and seals the grain);
Use the finish of your choice for the outside.

Now What? Or Where to Start

Now you have read about and seen the many discoveries that many turners have found through the past years. It is hard to truly understand all of this without putting many pieces of wood on the lathe and playing. Only then will much of this make more sense. This information is a foundation on which you can make and enjoy many forms.

Having the skill to turn a bead, a cove, and a v-cut reliably makes this type of turning much more fun and successful.

Start with simple forms to become used to cutting air wood and solid wood. Start in quadrant 1, arc type with parallel axes. Mark and save your experiments for reference. It takes time to really understand and predict what may happen.

6
TRICKS, FIXES, AND HINTS

Helpful Hints When Planning a Multi-Axis Project

Playful experimentation is a great strategy when learning multi-axis turning and even that must be planned. This work is confusing. Finding and using a systematic method to conceptualize multi-axis turning helps decrease the frequency of brain cramps. Also, it is important to know what possibilities and limits exist using the lathe. These strategies will help create a consistent and successful outcome.

It is hard for me to conceptualize three dimensional ideas, both in my head and on paper. Because of this, I do a lot of sketching on the lathe, usually on a smaller scale. Once I find ideas that interest me, I then use larger pieces of wood.

There are some factors that need to be in your mind before the wood is turned between centers. The type of outcome you want and the number of axes and the placement of the axes that you want to use are the two decisions that must be made initially.

First, turn the entire length of the wood to a cylinder, unless you have a reason to have square ends. If the ends are kept square, it is difficult to turn them later when the spindle is thin and fragile. If you plan to place an axis on the diagonal of the square, then leave it square.

Now decide the placement of the new axes and the type of outcome that you will make.

Press the spindle between centers on those axes so that when the spindle is fragile, the holes are already there and less pressure will be needed to secure the spindle. When the spindle is thin, the pressure required to imbed the points may *break* the spindle.

Number the axes, not only on the ends, but also on the outside of the spindle. I save at least one half inch on each end. This gives me adequate space to clearly mark the axes and enough wood to prevent end grain tear out. I use a permanent marker which is dark enough to see the numbers. Another opportunity exists for a mistake if the marks are not clear.

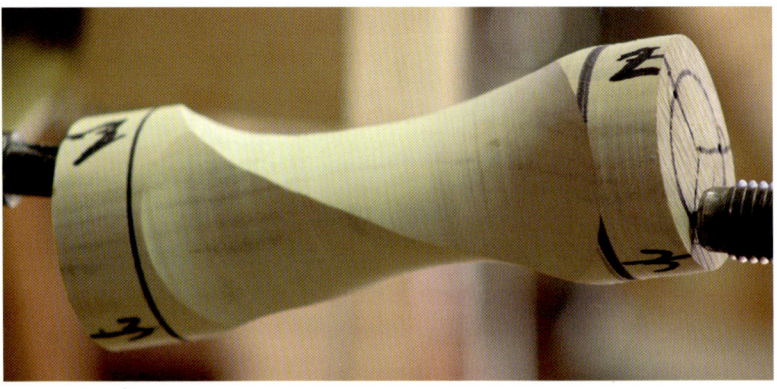

Decide on a *numbering system* and stick with it. Even when not distracted, it is easy to get the axes confused. My method of numbering the axes is to use the same numbers on each end and to go from the lowest number on the headstock end to the next highest on the tailstock end. If you have three parallel axes, the progression is 1-1, 2-2, 3-3. If you have three twisted axes, the progression is 1-2, 2-3, 3-1. (To make the twist go in the other direction, number the axes in the other direction.) This system works most of the time and when it fails to make sense, I figure out another system. See the photo on the opposite page.

Make notes *on* the project you are making and save it so it can be recreated. I usually could not figure out the notes I made on paper, so I started saving a sample spindle with the ends intact to remind me of the process. I have spent hours if not days trying to recreate something I had made but had forgotten to save a sample.

Sharp tools, good lighting, and the speed of the lathe are important factors when making a smooth cut. The tool has more time in the air rather than in the wood when the speed is slow. This increases the chance that the tool will bounce. To make smoother cuts, I increase the speed of the lathe to the highest point taking into account vibration and safety. At times the lathe may vibrate at one speed and will not vibrate at a higher speed. I think of this as harmonics.

When making an arc type spindle, the depth of cut becomes critical. The tool rest can be used as a reference point for the depth of the cut.

Sanding arc type spindles is a challenge, since the surfaces are curved and the edges are crisp lines. My goal as a turner is to sand as little as possible. This means the cut must be as smooth as possible. The arc type and any other non-round surface must be sanded by hand being careful to keep the edges crisp. I sometimes let the lathe hold the spindle while I sand it by hand. Cloth-backed sanding paper is thick enough to hold while sanding these surfaces. The circular type can be sanded with the lathe on. It helps to sand each axis before moving on to the next axis. The knuckles are in danger, so use caution.

Solutions to Random Problems

We all solve problems inherent in making things every day in our own shops. Here are a few solutions to problems that I've encountered along the way.

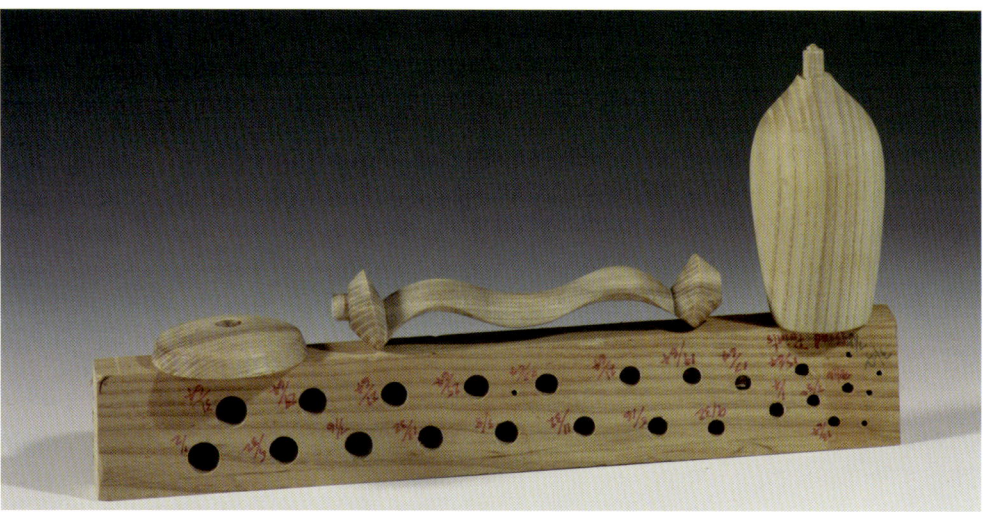

Mortise and tenon joinery

I made many goblets by attaching the cups to the stems and the stems to the bases using mortise and tenon joinery. My calipers never measured the correct diameter of the tenon. They were either a bit too tight or a bit too loose. This is my solution. I used every size drill bit to make a hole in a piece of hard wood and carefully label the size of each hole. Turn a random tenon on the bottom of the cup and then fit it in the tightest hole. Then use that drill bit to create the hole for the top of the stem. Use the lathe as the drill press.

After the hole is drilled, use the cone from the tail center to center the hole and make a final cut. This method successfully creates a centered hole. And the fit of this joint is consistently successful.

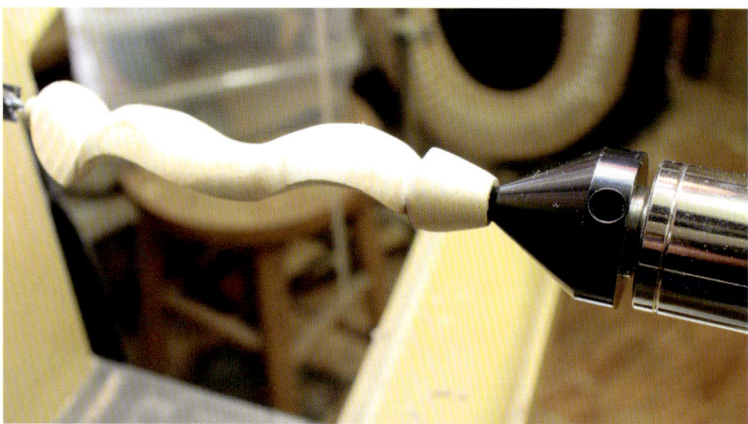

The uses of Plexiglas in multi-axis turning

Sometimes the drive center drills into the end grain making the piece spin rather than turn. A way to deal with this problem is to either soak the end grain with thin CA glue to stabilize the wood (after the points have been pressed deeply into the wood); or to use hot glue to keep the drive center from spinning out. Another solution is to drill holes into a piece of Plexiglas where the points from the drive center and tail centers will go. Then hot glue the Plexiglas to the end.

Plexiglas can also be used when making split turnings. It helps to glue Plexiglas to the ends of a split turning. (See the photo.)

The Plexiglas helps hold the pieces of glued-up wood together, prevents the points from the drive center and the tail center from splitting the glued-up wood, and helps secure the wood if the wood does not line up perfectly.

Inserts for candleholders

Candleholders often become sculptures. It is important for the inserts for the candles to be beautiful as well. Use the one-inch copper end caps from any hardware store. Turn a hole in a piece of oak deep enough for the copper insert to be placed in, but shallow enough for the rim to be hammered down and flattened. Coins can be used to adjust the height of the copper insert.

Drill a smaller hole through the bottom of the hole so the copper can be knocked out after the insert is formed.

Heat the copper with a torch until it has a red glow (anneal) to soften the metal. Then use a steel ball and a hammer to start rolling over the top. Use a ball peen hammer to finish flattening out the rim.

How to deal with vibration

Vibration is a huge factor when turning off balanced pieces of wood. Speed is one way to control the vibration. Another way to control vibration is to create a counterbalance.

There are many ways to create a counterbalance. This is a counterbalance that I use to help decrease the vibration while turning at a faster speed. It is a plywood disc with holes drilled into one side for fitting bolts used for the counterweight.

#2 morse taper extension

A #2 morse taper extension goes through the hole in the center. The four-jaw chuck can be loosened to balance the turning. The weights can be adjusted by adding or taking away the bolts.

Loosen the four-jaw chuck and hold the counterbalance so that gravity pulls the spindle down towards the bed of the lathe. Then rotate the counterbalance disc to put the weights on top or opposite of the weight of the spindle. Tighten the jaws and rotate the spindle. The weights should now offset the weight of the spindle. This must be adjusted each time an axis is changed or a catch is made that spins the spindle.

This system has allowed me to double the speed when turning an off-balanced spindle.

7
GALLERY

There are many ways to turn a beautiful object by using more than one axis when turning. This gallery includes the work of a few of the many artists who use the lathe as a primary tool.

Max Brosi

Max Brosi. 2015. Oak, 9.5" × 9.5".

Max Brosi. 2017. Oak, 7" × 7".

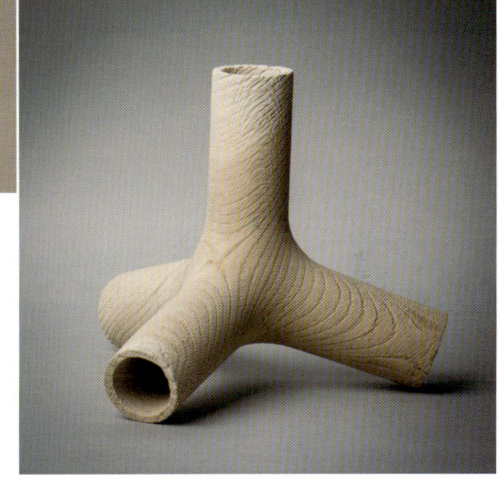

Max Brosi. 2015. Oak, 6.75" × 6.75" × 6.75".

Max Brosi. 2015. Oak, 9" × 6" × 8".

My work is in a constant state of evolution towards a more raw, honest, and calm aesthetic. Everything is in a state of transience: wood warps, metal corrodes. The result of these natural processes is a heightened aesthetic character in the material. The static becomes dynamic, the perfect becomes imperfect.

Many years of working with wood has taught me to design movement into my work by utilizing the natural tendency of wet oak to warp as it dries. Sandblasting reveals the hidden three-dimensional texture of the grain and rays.

I use simple geometric forms like cylinders and spheres, frequently turned over several axes on the lathe, to explore a visual concept and tell a story. This story can be a social or political commentary, or often just a simple exploration of form.

The distortion and texture of the warped wood breathes life into the starkness of geometric form and softens the brutality of cold, rusty steel. This tension between materials excites me.

Tom Crabb

Tom Crabb. *3 Pods*, 2002. Plum, hackberry, mesquite, 4" × 2.5".

Tom Crabb. *Pod*, 2005. Hackberry, turned on two axes, 4.5" h × 4" dia.

Tom Crabb. *Pod with Handle*, 2006. Hackberry, turned on two axes, handle was steam bent, 5" × 5" × 5.5" h.

Tom Crabb. *Turned Cube*, 1996. Ebony, turned on the bias using four axes, 7" × 7" × 3" h.

Luc Deroo

Luc Deroo. 2004. Walnut, 6" × 3.5".

Luc Deroo. American Oak Story Series, 2015. 8.27".

Luc Deroo. American Oak Story Series, 2015. 5.51".

Luc Deroo. *Butterfly,* 2016. Walnut, 9" × 4".

Luc Deroo. *Lunar Landscape # 13-1*, 2013. Maple and rusted steel, 7.5" and 5.5" dia.

Luc Deroo. *Pair # 5*, 2012. Brazilian tulipwood and European walnut, each 5" × 3".

Jean-François Escoulen

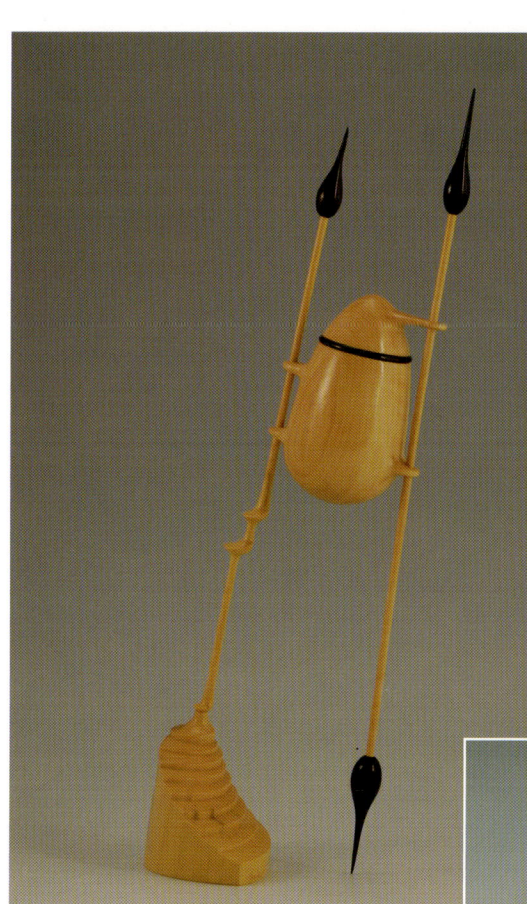

Jean-François Escoulen. Box in boxwood and ebony, 1996. 9.84" h. Made with Escoulen chuck number 1.

Jean-François Escoulen. *Getting Old*, 2009. 11.02" h. Made with Escoulen chuck number 3.

Jean-François Escoulen. Box in walnut, 2003. 13.78" h. Each piece is unique because I always look for new ideas by using my chucks. Boxes are for me an infinite source of creations.

Jean-François Escoulen. Box in pink ivory, 2010. The top is turned with two axes using Escoulen chuck number 1.

Peter Exton

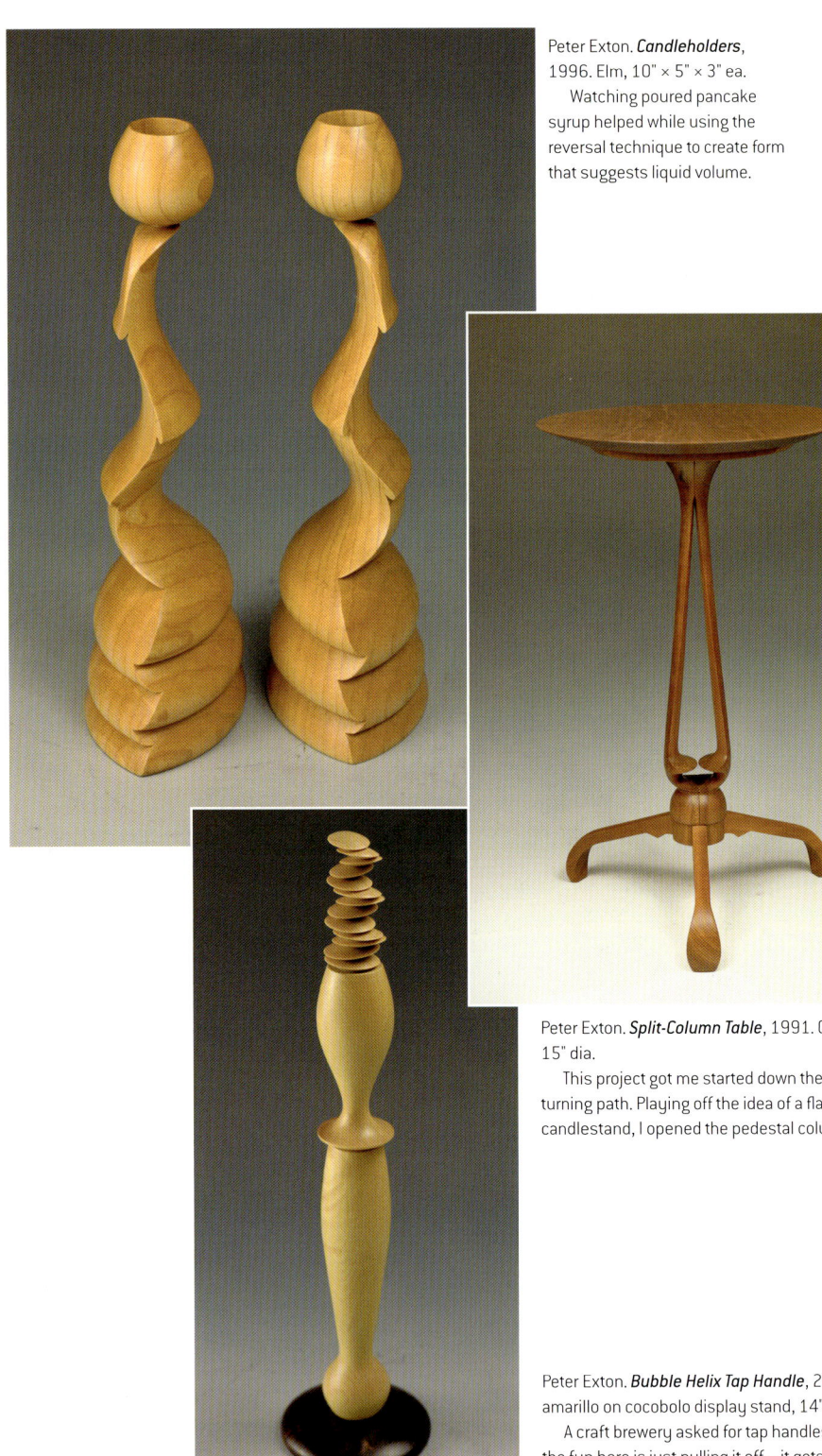

Peter Exton. *Candleholders*, 1996. Elm, 10" × 5" × 3" ea.
   Watching poured pancake syrup helped while using the reversal technique to create form that suggests liquid volume.

Peter Exton. *Split-Column Table*, 1991. Cherry, 25" × 15" dia.
   This project got me started down the reverse-turning path. Playing off the idea of a flame for a candlestand, I opened the pedestal column.

Peter Exton. *Bubble Helix Tap Handle*, 2016. Pau amarillo on cocobolo display stand, 14" × 2" dia.
   A craft brewery asked for tap handles. Much of the fun here is just pulling it off—it gets a bit tricky with the last "bubbles."

Peter Exton. *Curvatura*, 2016. Brazilian boxwood, cocobolo base, 11" × 4" dia.

The title means "curvature," for a piece that just piles up curve upon curve.

Peter Exton. *Sweet Green*, 1999. Maple, bubinga base, 20" × 3" dia. There are many things I like about this piece; it satisfies on many levels.

Michael Foster

Michael Foster. *Almost*, 2016. Gimlet burl, Macassar ebony base. 5.25" × 3.5" × 6".

Almost is a form that started as a true sphere that was then turned on an off-axis orientation. This pierced the sphere off center and removed a great amount of the original mass. The result was a sculptural object which retains the surface of the original sphere, yet has a presence that is quite remote from the feel of a sphere.

Michael Foster. *Event Horizon*, 2016. Cube and base made from Macassar ebony, 3.5" × 3.5" × 3.5".

Turned on six axes then the spirals carved into the resulting six faces.

Michael Foster. *Binary Black Hole*, 2014. Form: Cherry, India ink, and acrylics. Stand: Maple and acrylic. 13" h × 9" w × 2" d.

This is a minimal surface (called a modified Lawson surface) piece that takes inspiration from astrophysics in a rare and strange, but seemingly confirmed astral object, a binary black hole pair. Turned as a disc, then offset and turned on two more axes from each side.

Michael Foster. *Scherk Tower V*, 2015. Box elder burl, dyes, 3" × 3" × 12".
  Turned on thirty-four axes and carved to final form.

Michael Foster. *Tao Geometry*, 2011. Black ash burl. Stand: maple, stainless steel, pyrography. 8" dia. × 3" deep, 12" h on stand.
  Turned as an 8" × 3" disc, then offset and angled and turned from four mountings to achieve the perforations. Carved to final form. Pyrography detail on the stand and edge. Stain on one face, bleached on the other face, lacquer.

Michael Foster. *Trefoil*. Masur birch, lacquer. Stand: maple with India ink, 5" h × 7" dia.
  Turned on seven axes and carved to final form.

Keith Holt

Keith Holt. *Self Portrait*. Holly, 6" h × 4" w × 4" dia. In a private collection.

Keith Holt. *Spike*. Cherry, 5" h × 4" w × 4" dia. In a private collection.

Keith Holt. *Mr. Cellophane.* Holly and walnut, 4" w × 4" h × 5" dia. In a private collection.

Keith Holt. *Finding Fred*. Mahogany, stone paint; maple base, painted; steel. 14" h × 8" w × 6" dia. In a private collection.

When crafting a piece, I start with a general idea. I may even have a sketch or drawing. However, once on the lathe, the wood takes on a life of its own. The process of exploration is what makes creating these pieces so enjoyable. It is fascinating to see how the planes and angles combine to produce incredible surfaces and negative spaces.

The forms are created with an eccentric sphere jig that I designed. This jig gives a seemingly endless number of possibilities to explore.

Paul Hedman

Paul Hedman. *Whoville Fire Siren*, 2014. Spruce burl, turned on eleven axes. Carved, sandblasted, and bleached. 10" h × 14" dia.

This piece takes advantage of the circular grain patterns common in spruce burls.

Paul Hedman. *White Oak Tetrahedman.* White oak, 12" on each edge.

Turned on four axis, sandblasted, and finished with boiled linseed oil. These are the latest challenges the voices have given me. There were a lot of technical problems to solve in creating a jig to solidly hold these for turning. After several failures and partial successes I finally came up with something that works. The process sometimes means more to me than the product.

In the shop

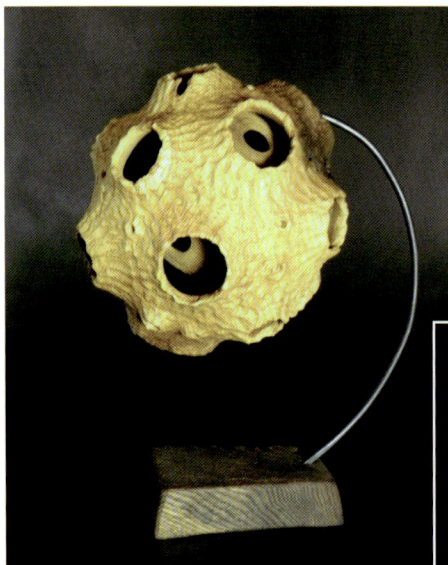

Paul Hedman. *White Oak Chinese Moon*. White oak, 8" dia.

Hollowed on twentysome axes, carved for texture, then sandblasted and finished with boiled linseed oil. This moon was hollowed and the inner moon hollowed through each of the craters, one at a time. By blocking some of the craters with hot-melt-glued-in plugs I was able to under cut the craters enough to free the inner moon. This series and the other geometrics were inspired by the incredible work of Claude Lethiecq, whom I was lucky enough to meet and spend time with in 2011.

Paul Hedman. *Acubeinacubeinacube*. White oak, 9" cube. Turned on six axes, sandblasted, and finished with boiled linseed oil. This is my take on a machinist cube, something of a test for metal machinists. The ones they make are usually 2" to 3" cubes and done on a mill or metal lathe. Mine is trued up and turned freehand on a wood lathe after cutting the rough cube oversized with a chainsaw.

Paul Hedman. *Chinese Moon Tetrahedman*, 2015. White oak, 15" on each edge.

Turned on four axes, with the moon being turned and hollowed on several more. The moon is bleached and the "tet" is finished with boiled linseed oil after sandblasting. This is one piece of wood that was turned in one piece. The moon has two layers with the inner one free of the outer. There were enough technical challenges in this to keep the voices working overtime.

Paul Hedman. *Double Tunneled Sphere*, 2014. White oak, 5".

This is a sphere with two offset flared tunnels intersecting at ninety degrees to each other. Blasted and bleached.

As you can tell I am enamored with texture in my turnings. The various woods I use have grain that shows up well when sandblasted and most of it also has great natural color. I sometimes alter the color by fuming, ebonizing, burning, bleaching, or combinations of these.

Michael Hosaluk

Tables, 23" h × 23" d × 14" w. Maple, acrylic paint and gel, charcoal, turned and sculpted, offset connectors, 2005. Photo: Trent Watts.

Male/Female, Maple, Largest 10" h × 6" d × 3.5" w. White gesso offset parts combined with turnings, glued together, 2007. Photo: Trent Watts.

Detail of below tables. Photo: Trent Watts.

Tables, 24" h × 23" d × 14" w. Maple, acrylic paint, and moulding paste, curly western maple, 2014. Photo: Trent Watts.

Offset candle stick demo, birch, 6" h × 3" dia. One offset axis to get people started with offset turning, 2015. Photo: Trent Watts.

Stoney Lamar. *Reliquary*, 1998. Blackwood, 23" × 8" × 8". Photo: Tim Barnwell.

Stoney Lamar. *All Dressed Up*, 2003.
Madrone burl, milk paint, steel,
22" × 14" × 10". Photo: Tim Barnwell.

Stoney Lamar. *Muse*, 1996. Madrone, 11" × 5" × 5". Photo: Tim
Barnwell.

Stoney Lamar. *Addicted to the Rhythm,* 1996. Cocobola, 10"
× 8" × 5". Photo: Tim Barnwell.

Art Liestman. *Tower for JP*. Big leaf maple, 15" × 5.5" × 4". Photo: Kenji Nagai.

Art Liestman. *Oroshi.* Big leaf maple, walnut, and steel wire, 6" × 6" × 3 3/8". Photo: Kenji Nagai.

Art Liestman. *H2*. Big leaf maple and walnut, 9 1/2" × 3" × 4 5/8". Photo: Kenji Nagai.

Art Liestman. *Inga.* Big leaf maple burl and ebony, 5.5" × 7" × 3.5". Photo: Kenji Nagai.

Derek Weidman

Derek Weidman. *Blue Claw*, 2015. Holly, acrylics, 14" h × 12" w × 10" d.

Derek Weidman. *Cecil*, 2016. Holly, acrylics, 30" h × 15" w × 17" d. Collection of Peabody Essex Museum.

I made this piece in response to the lion, Cecil, that was illegally poached the summer prior. The act of poaching was terrible, but the international response of so many people caring, and rallying behind preserving, protecting, and sharing the world with other life on this planet, was extremely moving to me.

Derek Weidman. *Woodpecker*, 2015. Holly, acrylics, 12" h × 10" w × 5" d.

My hands bruised from a day of creation. Hunks of wood spinning around voids, like some sort of black hole opening and closing in my studio. My body engaged in near dance, making a long cut, my foot sweeps across the floor in an arc, leaving a semicircle path on the ground now covered in wooden ribbons. There is a violent grace to the work, chunk chunk chunk, the chisel feeling air between hits, ethereal phantasms banging the tool, then, almost like a sunrise, a relief, fully engaged in something real, smoothly spiraling into the center.

Derek Weidman. *Pan*, 2008. Holly, ebony, metal, acrylics, 10" h × 6" w × 6" d.

    The work was originally going to be called *Shared Thought*, with an attempt to visually represent all living things on earth having a sameness. Late one night driving to a job I saw a family of raccoons trying desperately to cross a street. The mother crossed but the babies lagged behind, cars kept coming, and the mom was trying to cross back. The babies were slowly going into the street, so I just blocked traffic by turning my car sideways and they crossed safely. I thought *we all belong here* so vividly that night, and that feeling turned into this sculpture.

My goal when I first started really focusing on wood as my vehicle of expression was to try to build a visual language out of the indifferent, perfectly circular cuts of a wood lathe. Arcs, concentric tool marks, almost mechanical looking, were the vocabulary of the animal forms that began materializing from hunks of wood spinning rapidly in front of me. The process and the discovery was intoxicating. What would each animal look like through the distorting and oh-so-particular lens of a wood lathe? The process was violent and graceful, grain would tear, and rip; the work had a tension between the industrial and organic. . . .

Derek Weidman. *Saint of Bassou*, 2015. Holly, acrylics, 12" h × 9" w × 10" d.

I heard about these chimps in the Bossou region seeking out snares and disarming them with sticks. The chimps were also documented to have been seeing animals injured by snares and angrily shaking the snares in response. They behaved almost altruistically and compassionately, so I made this sculpture depicting them as saints, with a dissembled trap as a head piece or crown.

BIBLIOGRAPHY

Angerer, Sigi. Translated by Alan Lacer. "Angular Turning on the Lathe." *American Woodturner,* Summer 1998.

Crabb, Tom. "Something Different." *American Woodturner*, Spring 2007.

Darlow, Mike. *Woodturning Methods*. East Petersburg, PA: Fox Chapel, 2008.

Dill, Barbara. "Harmony." *American Woodturner*, October 2013.

———. "Multi Axis Spindle Turning: Further Exploration." *American Woodturner*, December 2011.

———. "Multi Axis Turning: A Systematic Approach." *American Woodturner*, Fall 2007.

———. "Multi Axis Turning Part 11: Turning a Goblet." *American Woodturner*, Winter 2007.

———. "Split Turning Series." *American Woodturner*, February 2010.

Exton, Peter. Photos of works in *American Woodturner*, Winter 2002.

———. "Turning Diamonds." *American Woodturner*, February 2010.

Foster, Michael. "Thinking Outside the Hollow Form." *American Woodturner*, April 2014.

Hopper, Ray. *Multi-Centre Woodturning*. Lewes, East Sussex: Guild of Master Craftsman Publications, 1992.

Lamar, Stoney. "Balancing on a Hard Edge." *American Woodturner,* June 2014.

Liestman, Art. "Beyond Round: Therming." *American Woodturner*, April 2010.

Sfirri, Mark. "Another View of Saskatoon." *American Woodturner*, December 1994.

———. "Multi-Axis Candlesticks: Making Offset Spindles That Keep Candles Straight." *American Woodturner*, March 1994.

———. "The Simple Turned Table Leg and a Variation. *American Woodturner*, June 1993.

Siegel, Jon. "Turning Dutch Foot Legs." *Fine Woodworking*, January/February 2009.

Verchot, Remi. "Turned Box Design: Varying Form by Reorienting the Box Parts." *American Woodturner*, Spring 1998.

"My interest is to systematically experiment with the many forms that can be turned on a lathe between centers."

Barbara Dill holds a master's degree in psychiatric nursing, and coordinated psychiatric aspects of emergency departments at Boston City Hospital and at Medical College of Virginia. She started turning wood nearly three decades ago. She studied with some of the world's finest turners early in her turning career at Arrowmont and has attended many classes, demonstrations, and hands-on sessions through the years. Always fascinated with multi-axis forms, she decided to focus her attention on multi-axis spindle turning in 2006.

Tired of running into dead ends with her candleholders, she decided to see if there was a way to sort out the confusion of this aspect of turning. If it's considered an obsession to wake up with a new "what if" most mornings, then she was obsessed.

Dill has written articles for *American Woodturner* and teaches at clubs and symposiums across the United States and Canada. She is a full-time studio artist in Rockville, Virginia.